I0821015

RENAE BRUMBAUGH GREEN

Clothe Your Heart in Prayer

ENCOURAGING DEVOTIONS FOR A WOMAN OF GOD

ISBN 979-8-89151-158-3

Cover design by Greg Jackson, ThinkPen Design

Published by Barbour Publishing, Inc., 1810 Barbour Drive, Uhrichsville, Ohio 44683, www.barbourbooks.com

Our mission is to inspire the world with the life-changing message of the Bible.

Printed in China.

Introduction

It's fun to wear a new outfit. When we get dressed up in clothes that fit well and are fashionable and appropriate, we hold our heads a little higher. Our clothes can lift our mood and make us feel like our best selves. If a bit of cloth and thread can do that, imagine what can happen when we clothe ourselves in God's best for us?

Prayer is a wardrobe essential for every Christian. The more time we spend with our Father, the higher we hold our heads. Our shoulders press back, and we're able to face our lives with the confidence of knowing we're daughters of the King. We are royalty! He adores us, and He wants nothing more than to walk through life with us, guiding each step and showering us with wisdom and strength, blessings and love along the way.

He Wants You

Rejoice always, pray continually, give thanks in all circumstances; for this is God's will for you in Christ Jesus.
1 THESSALONIANS 5:16–18 NIV

Have you ever wondered what God's will is for your life? If so, you're not alone. He created each of us with unique skills and purposes, but it all boils down to this: He made you because He wants a relationship with you. He adores you, and He wants to hang out with you all the time. He is completely *for* you. . . He's your biggest cheerleader and advocate. He wants to hear your thoughts, your dreams, and even your frustrations. One of the beautiful things about constant prayer is that it changes us. The more we talk to our Father, the more like Him we become. He gives us joy and gratitude for the lives He's blessed us with. Dive into His presence and talk to Him about everything. He will never be bored or annoyed or too busy for you.

THANK YOU FOR WANTING MY COMPANY, LORD. I'M SO GRATEFUL FOR YOUR LOVE.

Promise Keeper

But Abram said, "Sovereign Lord, what can you give me since I remain childless and the one who will inherit my estate is Eliezer of Damascus?" And Abram said, "You have given me no children; so a servant in my household will be my heir."

Genesis 15:2–3 NIV

God had promised that Abram's descendants would be as numerous as the stars. God always keeps His promises, but He doesn't always do it on our timeline. Since humans aren't always patient creatures, we can lose hope when prayers aren't answered immediately. We think He's forgotten, or we think we misunderstood Him.

That's how Abram felt. As time passed and Abram and his wife grew too old (by our standards) to have a child, Abram second-guessed God. He wondered if he should leave his stuff to a servant. But if we skip forward to chapter 21, we see that God meant exactly what He said. Sarah conceived and gave birth to Isaac. God will keep His promises to you as well.

REMEMBER YOUR PROMISES TO ME, LORD. I TRUST YOU, AND I BELIEVE.

Trust His Timing

And Abraham said to God, "If only Ishmael might live under your blessing!"
GENESIS 17:18 NIV

As time passed and Abram's patience waned, he kept talking to God. He kept the lines of communication open. But he and Sarah tried to manipulate God's plan when Abram, later called Abraham, slept with Sarah's servant, who gave birth to Ishmael. We do that too, don't we? When our prayers aren't answered as quickly as we want, or the answer isn't to our satisfaction, we try to help things along.

God doesn't force us to trust Him, but when we don't, we create more problems for ourselves. God didn't answer Abraham's prayer to make Ishmael his heir, because that wasn't God's will. He doesn't alter His promises to please us. But His plans are always far greater than anything we can come up with. Trust Him. His plans for you are good, and they're always worth the wait.

WAITING IS HARD, LORD. BUT I KNOW YOUR PLANS FOR ME ARE ALWAYS BEST, AND I TRUST YOUR TIMING.

An Overwhelming Task

Then he prayed, "Lord, God of my master Abraham, make me successful today, and show kindness to my master Abraham."
Genesis 24:12 NIV

When Abraham's son Isaac was a young man, his father realized there wasn't a suitable wife for him where they lived. Abraham sent his servant Eliezer to find a wife for Isaac among their relatives in their former land. That was quite a task! Eliezer must have felt overwhelmed. How was he to know the right woman? What if he failed?

Rather than panic, Eliezer asked God to show him what to do. He trusted God for success. When we feel overwhelmed, like there's no possible way we can accomplish what needs to be done, we can do what Eliezer did. We can say, "God, I can't do this on my own. I trust You for success."

I FEEL LIKE I'M BEING SET UP FOR FAILURE, LORD. I KNOW THE TASKS AHEAD ARE TOO DIFFICULT FOR ME. BUT NOTHING IS TOO DIFFICULT FOR YOU! GUIDE ME, AND HELP ME ACCOMPLISH WHAT NEEDS TO BE DONE.

A Difficult Relationship

Then Jacob prayed, "O God of my father Abraham, God of my father Isaac, LORD, you who said to me, 'Go back to your country and your relatives, and I will make you prosper.'. . . Save me, I pray, from the hand of my brother Esau, for I am afraid he will come and attack me, and also the mothers with their children."

GENESIS 32:9, 11 NIV

Years before, Jacob had fled his home after cheating his brother, Esau, out of his birthright and blessing. Now he wanted to return home—at God's bidding—but he was afraid Esau would take revenge on him and his family. He couldn't control Esau's attitude or actions, so he asked God to prepare the way. God gave Jacob wisdom and softened Esau's heart. Ask God to heal your relationships, to give you wisdom and soften others' hearts.

YOU KNOW THE HISTORY OF MY RELATIONSHIPS, LORD. I WANT THERE TO BE PEACE. GIVE ME WISDOM FOR HOW TO TREAT THOSE PEOPLE, AND SOFTEN THEIR HEARTS TOWARD ME.

When God Says No

Moses again pleaded, "Lord, please! Send anyone else."
EXODUS 4:13 NLT

It's encouraging to read about people whose prayers were answered the way they wanted. But when Moses asked God to choose someone else to face Pharaoh and lead the Israelites to freedom, He said no. He did, however, give Moses a helper in his brother, Aaron.

God chose Moses for this. As an infant, Moses was supposed to die. Instead, he was found and adopted by Pharaoh's daughter and brought up in the palace as a prince. He was highly educated and was used to dealing with important people. God knew Moses had what it took—He had created Moses, after all! If God doesn't answer your prayer the way you want, He will provide you with the skills and resources to do what you've been called to do.

I KNOW YOU'VE CALLED ME TO DO THIS THING, LORD, BUT I DON'T FEEL CAPABLE, AND IT'S OUT OF MY COMFORT ZONE. I TRUST YOU TO EQUIP ME TO DO WHAT YOU'VE CALLED ME TO.

What Lies Ahead

One day Moses said to the LORD, "You have been telling me, 'Take these people up to the Promised Land.' But you haven't told me whom you will send with me. You have told me, 'I know you by name, and I look favorably on you.' If it is true that you look favorably on me, let me know your ways. . . ."
The LORD replied, "I will personally go with you, Moses, and I will give you rest—everything will be fine for you."

EXODUS 33:12–14 NLT

Sometimes we have a general idea of what God wants us to do, but we don't know the specifics. That can be frustrating. It's okay to share those frustrations with God. Moses asked God to let him know His plans. God's response was an assurance: "I'll be with you. It will be okay."

I TRUST YOU, LORD. BUT IT'S HARD WHEN I DON'T KNOW WHERE I'M GOING. THANK YOU FOR THE PROMISE OF YOUR PRESENCE. I KNOW IT WILL ALL WORK OUT FOR MY GOOD, BECAUSE I KNOW YOU LOVE ME.

Prayers for Blessings

"The Lord bless you and keep you; the Lord make his face to shine upon you and be gracious to you; the Lord lift up his countenance upon you and give you peace."
Numbers 6:24–26 ESV

Aaron, Moses' brother, prayed this blessing over the Israelites. He loved his nation, and he wanted God's goodness to follow them. This is a beautiful prayer to pray for all those we love, whether it's our family, our friends, or our country. God did bless the Israelite people, because He loved them even more than Aaron did. When we pray in agreement with God—when we ask Him to do something He's already promised to do—we can know He will answer. And we'll receive even greater blessings, because our prayers allow us to participate in God's great plan.

FATHER, I KNOW YOU LOVE THE PEOPLE IN MY HEART EVEN MORE THAN I DO. I PRAY YOUR BLESSINGS ON THEM. THANK YOU FOR LETTING ME TAKE PART IN THOSE BLESSINGS THROUGH THE ACT OF PRAYER.

In His Presence

And whenever the ark set out, Moses said,
"Arise, O L*ORD, and let your enemies be scattered,*
and let those who hate you flee before you."
And when it rested, he said, "Return, O L*ORD,*
to the ten thousand thousands of Israel."
NUMBERS 10:35–36 ESV

As the Israelites traveled toward the Promised Land, the ark of the covenant was the physical representation of God's presence and protection. Moses prayed for God to scatter their enemies and keep them safe. God did protect them during the times the Israelites' hearts were devoted to God. But when Israel strayed and chose to live in sin, they moved away from God's protection. Remember, God never changes. If you don't feel His presence, take a look at your own life to see if you're the one who pulled away.

I KNOW YOU ARE GOOD, FATHER. I KNOW YOU ARE UNCHANGING. YOU PROMISED TO NEVER LEAVE ME, BUT SOMETIMES, WITHOUT REALIZING IT, I LEAVE YOU. SHOW ME WHAT I MAY BE DOING TO PULL AWAY FROM YOU. I NEED YOUR PRESENCE.

Accepting Help

Moses heard the people weeping throughout their clans, everyone at the door of his tent. And the anger of the LORD blazed hotly, and Moses was displeased. Moses said to the LORD, "Why have you dealt ill with your servant? And why have I not found favor in your sight, that you lay the burden of all this people on me?"

NUMBERS 11:10–11 ESV

God put Moses in charge of the Israelites. Moses did what many of us do—he tried to do everything himself. But leadership only works if you *lead*. No one is supposed to do everything on their own. God answered Moses' prayer by appointing some of the elders to help. When the task ahead is too large for you, ask God to send helpers.

I OFTEN FALL INTO THE TRAP OF DOING EVERYTHING ON MY OWN. IT SEEMS EASIER THAN TRAINING SOMEONE ELSE OR TRUSTING THEM TO DO WHAT'S NEEDED. FORGIVE ME FOR MY PRIDE. PLEASE SEND HELPERS, AND GIVE ME HUMILITY TO ACCEPT HELP.

Remind God of His Promises

But Moses said, "The people among whom I am number six hundred thousand on foot, and you have said, 'I will give them meat, that they may eat a whole month!' Shall flocks and herds be slaughtered for them, and be enough for them? Or shall all the fish of the sea be gathered together for them, and be enough for them?"

NUMBERS 11:21–22 ESV

The Israelites were hungry. Moses was beside himself, wondering how he was supposed to feed over six hundred thousand people. He reminded God of His promise to feed them and wondered how such a thing could happen. God always keeps His promises, and He loves it when we remind Him of them. That shows we were paying attention! God provided the Israelites with manna to eat, and they were never hungry for the rest of their journey through the desert.

THANK YOU FOR YOUR PROMISES,
FATHER. I KNOW YOU ARE FAITHFUL.
RIGHT NOW, I CLAIM YOUR
SPECIFIC PROMISE TO ________.
I TRUST YOU WITH THE OUTCOME.

God's patience
is long and
His mercy is quick.

Admitting When We're Wrong

The people came to Moses and said, "We sinned when we spoke against the LORD and against you. Pray that the LORD will take the snakes away from us." So Moses prayed for the people.

NUMBERS 21:7 NIV

Once the people were out of Egypt and no longer in danger of being captured, they quickly forgot all God had done for them. They began to complain about how tired and hungry they were. Their complaints angered God, and He sent poisonous snakes! At that point, they repented and asked Moses to intercede for them. God's patience is long and His mercy is quick. He provided a way for the Israelites to survive the snake bites. He doesn't take pleasure in punishment. . .He longs for our repentance.

I KNOW THE TROUBLES I FACE ARE OFTEN THE RESULT OF MY OWN POOR CHOICES. I'M SORRY FOR DISOBEYING YOU, LORD. I KNOW I WAS WRONG. I NEED YOUR MERCY. PLEASE RESCUE ME FROM THE CONSEQUENCES, OR CARRY ME THROUGH THEM WITH YOUR GRACE.

Consequences of Sin

"Let the Lord, the God of the spirits of all flesh, appoint a man over the congregation who shall go out before them and come in before them, who shall lead them out and bring them in, that the congregation of the Lord may not be as sheep that have no shepherd."

Numbers 27:16–17 ESV

Moses was a good, godly leader. But he wasn't perfect! Once, he tried to take credit for bringing water from a rock instead of doing as God had asked him. Because of Moses' disobedience, God decided that Moses would never enter the Promised Land. He would see it from a distance, but he'd die before entering. Moses accepted this consequence of his own poor choice and prayed that God would provide a new leader for His people. God provided the right man—Joshua. Sin has consequences, but God's love never changes.

I KNOW MY POOR CHOICES HAVE AFFECTED MY LIFE AND THE LIVES OF OTHERS. I'M THANKFUL FOR YOUR FORGIVENESS. PLEASE PROVIDE HEALING AND PROSPERITY FOR THE PEOPLE I'VE HURT. I TRUST YOUR GOODNESS.

Another Chance

"And I prayed to the Lord, 'O Lord God, do not destroy your people and your heritage, whom you have redeemed through your greatness, whom you have brought out of Egypt with a mighty hand.'"
Deuteronomy 9:26 ESV

God worked so many miracles for the Israelites, you'd think they'd never forget. But our memories can be short. While Moses was on Mount Sinai communing with God, the people created a golden calf and began to worship it. God was so angry and hurt that He was going to destroy them.

But Moses reminded God of all He'd done and begged God to give them another chance. God heard, and He relented. When we see those we love turning away from God, we can pray! Prayer is a powerful tool. We can change God's heart with our earnest, sincere pleas.

IT BREAKS MY HEART TO SEE THOSE I LOVE TURN AGAINST YOU. I KNOW IT BREAKS YOUR HEART EVEN MORE. PLEASE DON'T GIVE UP ON THEM. BRING THEM BACK TO YOU.

Agreeing with God

On the day the Lord gave the Amorites over to Israel, Joshua said to the Lord in the presence of Israel: "Sun, stand still over Gibeon, and you, moon, over the Valley of Aijalon."

JOSHUA 10:12 NIV

Several kings united to destroy Joshua's allies in Gibeon because they wanted to weaken Israel's chances of success. Joshua and his forces rushed to the Gibeonites' aid, but he knew he needed God's help. He prayed that God would cause time to be on their side—to stand still—so they could defeat the enemy. God had already determined that Israel would defeat its enemies, so He answered Joshua's unusual prayer. God will always answer prayers when they align with His predetermined will.

FATHER, I KNOW I HAVE NO RIGHT TO ORDER YOU AROUND OR DEMAND ANYTHING FROM YOU. BUT I PRAY NOW, AGREEING WITH YOUR DESIRES. I KNOW THAT NOTHING IS IMPOSSIBLE FOR YOU, AND I TRUST YOU COMPLETELY. PAVE THE WAY FOR YOUR WILL TO PLAY OUT IN MY LIFE.

Facing Change

After the death of Joshua, the Israelites asked the Lord,
"Who of us is to go up first to fight against the Canaanites?"
Judges 1:1 NIV

From the time we're born, we go through a steady stream of changes, one after another. But even though we've all experienced it, most of us don't like change. The Israelites were no different. When Joshua died, they felt some anxiety and confusion over who would lead them into battle. Instead of arguing about it, they asked God. He answered quickly, telling them that the tribe of Judah would take the lead and that they would win. When we face change, we can trust God for guidance. He may only show us the next step, but we can take it in faith, knowing He'll lead us each step of the way.

I'M FACING SOME CHANGES IN MY LIFE, LORD, AND I DON'T KNOW WHAT TO DO NEXT. WILL YOU SHOW ME? MAKE YOUR WAY CLEAR SO I DON'T MESS UP. I TRUST YOU COMPLETELY.

When God Calls

"Pardon me, my lord," Gideon replied, "but how can I save Israel? My clan is the weakest in Manasseh, and I am the least in my family."

JUDGES 6:15 NIV

The Israelites were stubborn and rebellious. God handed them over to their enemies, the Midianites, to let them see what life without Him would be like. When they finally repented and asked God to rescue them, He spoke to a humble farmer named Gideon and told him he'd save the Israelites. Understandably, Gideon questioned this calling: "I'm nobody important. How can I save Israel?"

God's answer was simple. "I will be with you."

Has God called you to do something you don't feel qualified for? That's okay. If He's called you to something, He will equip you. And He will never leave you to do it alone.

FATHER, I FEEL OUT OF MY DEPTH. BUT IF I FELT QUALIFIED, I MIGHT NOT LEAN ON YOU LIKE I SHOULD. SHOW ME WHAT TO DO, LORD. I WILL FOLLOW YOUR LEAD.

When We Make a Mess

But the Israelites said to the Lord, "We have sinned.
Do with us whatever you think best, but please rescue us now."
Judges 10:15 NIV

Time and again, the Israelites found themselves in trouble because of their own rebellion. They'd sin, moving away from God. The consequences of their sin would become unbearable, and they'd beg God to save them. God would come to their rescue, and they'd live in obedience for a little while before the cycle continued.

We may shake our heads at the Israelites, but they're not so different from us. We're human, and humans have a sin nature. We often choose to disobey God and ignore the consequences. But God loves His children. He is patient, kind, and merciful. He won't always remove the natural consequences of our sin, but He will always be there when we call for Him. He will always welcome us home.

I'VE MESSED UP AGAIN, LORD.
I'M SO SORRY. PLEASE RESCUE ME
FROM THIS MESS I'VE MADE.

A Foolish Promise

And Jephthah made a vow to the LORD: "If you give the Ammonites into my hands, whatever comes out of the door of my house to meet me when I return in triumph from the Ammonites will be the LORD's, and I will sacrifice it as a burnt offering."

JUDGES 11:30–31 NIV

God granted Jephthah's request to defeat the Ammonites, because that was part of His plan. When Jephthah made his bargain with God, he probably thought a servant or pet would be the first he'd see. But the first to greet Jephthah was his daughter, his only child.

Scholars agree that the Hebrew conjunction for *and* is also used as *or*. He'd have sacrificed (killed) an animal, but instead, he dedicated his daughter to God's service. This meant she'd remain a virgin and he'd have no grandchildren. Many feel this was a foolish bargain to make. When you pray, be careful not to promise things you're not willing to follow through with.

I KNOW YOU ALWAYS KEEP YOUR WORD, LORD. HELP ME KEEP MY WORD TOO.

Humble Prayers

Then Samson prayed to the LORD, "Sovereign LORD, remember me. Please, God, strengthen me just once more, and let me with one blow get revenge on the Philistines for my two eyes."
JUDGES 16:28 NIV

Samson addressed God only once before in his written story. The first time, he killed a bunch of Philistines with a donkey's jawbone. He credited God, but he was also a little prideful. In this verse, Samson had been captured and blinded. He approached God from a place of total humility. Samson knew that God was his only hope. God answered Samson's prayer because it was His plan to defeat the Philistines.

God longs for humility in our prayers. He wants us to pray, knowing He's our only help. If we pray as a last resort or as a backup plan, we're really saying, "I think I've got this, but just in case, would You be on standby?" God is all-powerful, and He wants all the credit for what He does.

HELP ME, GOD. YOU'RE THE
ONLY ONE WHO CAN.

Why?

"Lord, God of Israel," they cried, "why has this happened to Israel? Why should one tribe be missing from Israel today?"

Judges 21:3 NIV

The question *Why?* is probably one of the most common prayers. We don't understand so many things in this life. They don't seem fair. They don't make sense. But God didn't give the Israelites a reason, and He doesn't always give us a reason.

That's where faith comes in. God is God. He's always good. And He's always working on our behalf. But because He is God, He's under no obligation to explain Himself. He doesn't have to reveal His plan. He's not required to tell us what He's doing or why He's doing it.

Even so, we can trust His goodness. We can trust that His plan is filled with love, kindness, mercy, and grace. And when we don't understand, we can know He's right there with us, holding us close, loving us through the pain.

**HELP ME UNDERSTAND, LORD.
BUT EVEN IF I NEVER KNOW WHY,
I TRUST YOUR GOODNESS.**

Trust His Plan

And she made this vow: "O Lord of Heaven's Armies, if you will look upon my sorrow and answer my prayer and give me a son, then I will give him back to you. He will be yours for his entire lifetime, and as a sign that he has been dedicated to the Lord, his hair will never be cut."

1 Samuel 1:11 NLT

Hannah desperately wanted a child, but at this point, she was barren. She prayed and wept so earnestly that the priest thought she was drunk. God saw her humility and granted her a son. She kept her promise and dedicated that son—Samuel—to God's service. After that, God blessed her with three more sons and two daughters.

It's difficult to understand why some things happen, but God always has a plan. If it had been easy for Hannah to have children, she probably wouldn't have dedicated her oldest child to God. Samuel went on to be Israel's last judge and first prophet. Whatever's happening, trust His plan!

I TRUST YOUR PLAN, LORD.

Prayer of Praise

Then Hannah prayed: "My heart rejoices in the Lord! The Lord has made me strong. Now I have an answer for my enemies; I rejoice because you rescued me. No one is holy like the Lord! There is no one besides you; there is no Rock like our God."

1 Samuel 2:1–2 NLT

God answered Hannah's prayer for a son, and this prayer of praise was her response. She was truly overwhelmed with God's goodness, and she told Him so. Psalm 22:3 says God inhabits the praises of His people. Our praise is His address! That's where He lives.

We often cry out to God when we face hardship, then forget about Him when things go well. But God longs for our praise. What can you praise God for today? Tell Him. Tell others. By praising Him, you ensure His presence in each moment of your life.

THERE ARE SO MANY THINGS TO PRAISE YOU FOR, FATHER. TOO MANY TO COUNT! YOU'RE AMAZING. THERE IS NONE LIKE YOU—NO ONE CAN COMPARE. THANK YOU FOR BEING MY GOD.

God inhabits the praises of His people. Our praise is His address! That's where He lives.

When God Doesn't Answer

So Saul asked God, "Should we go after the Philistines? Will you help us defeat them?" But God made no reply that day.

1 SAMUEL 14:37 NLT

Saul, Israel's king, asked God for guidance. But Saul lived in sin. Sin was a daily, rebellious choice for him. He approached God only when he needed help, and he spent the rest of his time doing what he wanted.

God had Saul's number. If we show up only when we need something from Him, we might want to rethink our relationship. God longs for our hearts. He wants us to sincerely love Him. We can go to God anytime and tell Him we're sorry and we want to change, and ask Him for help. But when we make a habit of ignoring Him until we're in trouble, He may decide to stay quiet for a while.

I'M SORRY FOR MY SINFULNESS, LORD. I KNOW I DON'T DESERVE ANYTHING FROM YOU. BUT I NEED YOU! HELP ME TURN FROM MY SIN AND LIVE FOR YOU.

Act, Don't React

One day news came to David that the Philistines were
at Keilah stealing grain from the threshing floors.
David asked the Lord, *"Should I go and attack them?"*
"Yes, go and save Keilah," the Lord *told him.*
1 Samuel 23:1–2 NLT

When faced with a difficult situation, David didn't react immediately. Instead, he asked God for guidance. Though he was surely angered to learn of the Philistines' behavior, David didn't let that anger determine his path. He sought God's wisdom first. Later, when people questioned his decision to fight the Philistines, David didn't cave in to peer pressure. He went back to God again, just to be sure. David saw victory because he sought God's guidance and did what He told him to do.

Do you face a frustrating situation? Does something make you angry? Don't react. Instead, seek God, and follow His wisdom.

YOU KNOW WHAT I'M DEALING WITH, LORD. IF I ACT ON MY EMOTIONS, I'LL SURELY SAY OR DO SOMETHING I'LL REGRET. GUIDE ME. GIVE ME YOUR WISDOM. SHOW ME WHAT TO DO.

Fight, Flight, or Pray

Then David asked the Lord, "Should I chase after this band of raiders? Will I catch them?" And the Lord told him, "Yes, go after them. You will surely recover everything that was taken from you!"
1 Samuel 30:8 NLT

David and his men left home to try to help some allies, only to be sent back. When they got home, their town had been raided. The enemy burned everything to the ground and kidnapped all the women and children. Even though David was desperate with emotion, he didn't respond rashly. He sought God's wisdom and guidance before taking action.

David and his men found their families and recovered them, along with all the spoils the raiders had stolen. When you're overwhelmed, when your circumstances force you into fight-or-flight mode, take a moment. Breathe deeply, and remember that nothing catches God by surprise. Ask Him to show you the next step, and the next, and the next.

I'M TERRIFIED. I NEED YOUR WISDOM, GUIDANCE, AND POWER. I TRUST YOU, AND I'LL DO WHATEVER YOU SAY.

Consequences

But after he had taken the census, David's conscience began to bother him. And he said to the Lord, *"I have sinned greatly by taking this census. Please forgive my guilt,* Lord, *for doing this foolish thing."*
2 Samuel 24:10 NLT

Why was it wrong for David to take a census? While counting the people wasn't wrong, it's clear David knew he'd offended God. Many scholars believe David counted people so he could brag about how big his army was, while God was clear in Exodus that people were to be counted so they could give an appropriate amount of money to support the temple and its workers. God wanted the census to remind people of His sovereignty. David's use of the census sent the message that people should trust in numbers, not God.

David asked for and received forgiveness, but he (and his people) still had to deal with the consequences of his sin.

HELP ME REMEMBER THAT SIN HAS CONSEQUENCES, LORD. I DON'T WANT TO HURT THE PEOPLE I LOVE BECAUSE OF MY OWN REBELLION.

All Your Heart

"Give your servant therefore an understanding mind to govern your people, that I may discern between good and evil, for who is able to govern this your great people?"
1 Kings 3:9 ESV

Young Solomon loved God with all his heart. God was so pleased with Solomon that He told him to ask for whatever he wanted, and God would grant it. Solomon could have asked for money or fame, but he didn't. He asked God for wisdom to help him lead his people. God was so pleased with Solomon's request that He granted wisdom, money, and fame! God gave him everything a young man could want.

Solomon loved God, but if you know the rest of his story, you know he was far from perfect. God uses imperfect people. The goal isn't perfection. . .it's to love God with all your heart.

I HAVE SO MANY FLAWS, LORD. I'M NOT SURE HOW YOU COULD EVER USE ME. BUT I LOVE YOU WITH ALL THAT I AM. I AM YOURS.

Even When It's Hard

And he cried to the L*ORD*, *"O* L*ORD* *my God, have you brought calamity even upon the widow with whom I sojourn, by killing her son?" Then he stretched himself upon the child three times and cried to the* L*ORD*, *"O* L*ORD* *my God, let this child's life come into him again."*

1 KINGS 17:20–21 ESV

Elijah asked a poor widow for food, and the woman shared that she didn't have enough to feed herself and her son. Elijah promised her that if she fed him, God would make sure they had plenty. Sure enough, her food never ran out! A while later, that woman's son died, and Elijah begged God to bring the child back to life. God did!

Some of God's ways are hard for us to understand. But this one thing we know: God listens to people who obey Him even when it's hard. What hard thing do you face? Like the poor widow, obey Him, even when obedience doesn't make sense.

HELP ME OBEY YOU EVEN WHEN IT'S HARD.

Light the Fire

Elijah the prophet came near and said, "O Lord, God of Abraham, Isaac, and Israel, let it be known this day that you are God in Israel, and that I am your servant, and that I have done all these things at your word. Answer me, O Lord, answer me, that this people may know that you, O Lord, are God."
1 Kings 18:36–37 ESV

Ahab was a wicked king who encouraged idol worship in Israel. Elijah confronted Ahab and issued a challenge. All the pagan prophets were to set up a sacrifice for their gods and then call on those gods to set fire to it. They did, and what a show they put on! But it never caught fire, because those idols were just wood and metal. They weren't real.

Elijah drenched his own firewood with water and asked God to prove Himself. Sure enough, the wood caught fire. Elijah's prayer wasn't for himself. It was for people to know and acknowledge God.

LIGHT FIRE TO MY LIFE SO OTHERS WILL KNOW YOU'RE REAL.

A Nap and a Snack

But he himself went a day's journey into the wilderness and came and sat down under a broom tree. And he asked that he might die, saying, "It is enough; now, O LORD, take away my life, for I am no better than my fathers."

1 KINGS 19:4 ESV

God worked through Elijah in powerful ways. Yet when the king's wife, Jezebel, threatened to kill Elijah, he fled for his life. He wondered if anything he'd done for God was even worth it. He didn't plan to kill himself, but he begged God to end his life for him. It's safe to say he was discouraged and depressed. In the next verse, Elijah went to sleep. Then an angel woke him up and gave him something to eat and drink.

God never leaves us alone in our sadness. He's right there, watching over us when we sleep and providing for our physical and emotional needs.

I DON'T KNOW IF I CAN GO ON, LORD. I NEED YOUR REST AND PROVISION RIGHT NOW.

Open My Eyes

He said, "Do not be afraid, for those who are with us are more than those who are with them." Then Elisha prayed and said, "O Lord, please open his eyes that he may see." So the Lord opened the eyes of the young man, and he saw, and behold, the mountain was full of horses and chariots of fire all around Elisha.

2 Kings 6:16–17 ESV

The king of Syria sent soldiers to capture Elisha, because he didn't like how God used the prophet. When Elisha's servant saw the army, he was afraid. Elisha gave him the same reminder we all need sometimes. God's army is stronger than any earthly enemy we face. Even when we can't see it, God is working on our behalf in powerful ways.

JUST AS YOU OPENED THIS YOUNG MAN'S EYES TO SEE YOUR WARRIORS SURROUNDING THE ENEMY, OPEN MY SPIRITUAL EYES. EVEN IF I CAN'T PHYSICALLY SEE YOU, I KNOW YOU'RE WORKING. I KNOW YOU LOVE ME AND YOU'RE FIGHTING FOR ME.

The Prayers of the Righteous

"Now, O Lord, please remember how I have walked before you in faithfulness and with a whole heart, and have done what is good in your sight." And Hezekiah wept bitterly.

2 Kings 20:3 ESV

Hezekiah was a righteous king who tried to please God in all he did. He got rid of all forms of pagan worship in Israel, which was no small task. He became very ill, and the prophet Isaiah told him he'd die. But Hezekiah wasn't ready to die, and he uttered the prayer above. Soon after, Isaiah came back and told Hezekiah that God changed His mind and would give him more time. James 5:16 tells us the prayers of a righteous person are powerful and effective. All sincere prayer is powerful. But when we love God with our whole heart, our prayers hold more weight than the prayers of those who pray only when they're in trouble.

THANK YOU FOR HEARING MY PRAYERS, FATHER. I LOVE YOU WITH ALL I AM, AND I WANT TO SERVE YOU ONLY.

Jabez prayed boldly,
asking God for
exactly what he wanted.

Model Prayer

There was a man named Jabez who was more honorable than any of his brothers. His mother named him Jabez because his birth had been so painful. He was the one who prayed to the God of Israel, "Oh, that you would bless me and expand my territory! Please be with me in all that I do, and keep me from all trouble and pain!" And God granted him his request.

1 CHRONICLES 4:9–10 NLT

Based on this account, Jabez didn't have a chance at a happy life. His mother named him "Pain!" Yet like all of us, Jabez made his choices. He loved God and tried to honor Him in all he did. He prayed boldly, asking God for exactly what he wanted. His model is a good template for our own prayers. First he asked for blessing. Next, he asked for influence. Finally, he asked for God's presence and protection in his life.

FATHER, BLESS ME. GIVE ME INFLUENCE SO I CAN POINT OTHERS TO YOU. STAY WITH ME AND PROTECT ME ALWAYS.

Hope for the Powerless

Then Asa cried out to the Lord his God, "O Lord, no one but you can help the powerless against the mighty! Help us, O Lord our God, for we trust in you alone. It is in your name that we have come against this vast horde. O Lord, you are our God; do not let mere men prevail against you!"

2 Chronicles 14:11 NLT

Asa was a good, righteous king of Judah who loved God with all his heart. One day, Zerah of Ethiopia attacked Judah. Zerah had a million-man army and three hundred chariots. Asa must have been terrified! But he took his fear to God in prayer. God is more powerful than the mightiest army, and He cares for those who seek Him.

What circumstance feels hopeless and overpowering to you? Take your fears to God. He is all-powerful, and He loves you more than you can imagine.

LORD, I FEEL POWERLESS. NO ONE BUT YOU CAN HELP ME. I TRUST YOU ALONE, AND I CAN'T WAIT TO SEE WHAT YOU'LL DO.

First Response

Praise the Lord, the God of our ancestors, who made the king want to beautify the Temple of the Lord in Jerusalem! And praise him for demonstrating such unfailing love to me by honoring me before the king, his council, and all his mighty nobles! I felt encouraged because the gracious hand of the Lord my God was on me. And I gathered some of the leaders of Israel to return with me to Jerusalem.

EZRA 7:27–28 NLT

Ezra was a priest who, more than anything, wanted to restore the temple and lead people to truly worship God. He received a letter from the king giving him permission to do these things and instructing others to follow Ezra's orders in accomplishing this. Ezra's first response was to praise God for making this happen. This shows that praise was a natural response for him. Like Ezra, we need to make praise our first, natural response, for *every good thing* comes from God.

I PRAISE YOU, LORD, FOR YOUR GOODNESS. THANK YOU FOR ALL YOU'VE DONE FOR ME.

Responding to Bullies

For they all wanted to frighten us, thinking, "Their hands will drop from the work, and it will not be done." But now, O God, strengthen my hands.

NEHEMIAH 6:9 ESV

Nehemiah led people to rebuild the wall around Jerusalem. When his enemies heard they were nearly finished, they began to threaten and bully Nehemiah. They thought that by picking a fight, they'd slow down the work. When faced with bullies, many of us enter a fight-or-flight mode. We stop everything to deal with the bully, which is exactly what they want. Nehemiah was wise enough to ignore the enemies' slanderous words. Instead of reacting in fear and anger, he asked God to give him strength.

What bullies do you face? Don't let them keep you from fulfilling your purpose. Take the problem to God, and ask Him to strengthen and protect you.

IT'S HARD TO IGNORE GOSSIP, SLANDER, AND BULLYING THREATS. GIVE ME WISDOM TO RESPOND CORRECTLY, AND GIVE ME STRENGTH TO KEEP LIVING OUT YOUR PURPOSE FOR MY LIFE.

Confession and Praise

Then the leaders of the Levites—Jeshua, Kadmiel, Bani, Hashabneiah, Sherebiah, Hodiah, Shebaniah, and Pethahiah—called out to the people: "Stand up and praise the Lord *your God, for he lives from everlasting to everlasting!" Then they prayed: "May your glorious name be praised! May it be exalted above all blessing and praise!"*

Nehemiah 9:5 NLT

Just prior to this verse, the Israelites confessed their *many* sins to God. They mourned and fasted and wore sackcloth and put dirt on their faces—all acts that conveyed their sincere sorrow. But then the Levites—the spiritual leaders—told them to stand up and praise God!

There is a time for mourning and a time for praise. Confession—realizing how much we've offended God—prepares us for a true attitude of praise. Repentance makes us aware that God owes us nothing, but He showers us with good things anyway because of His love.

I'M SO SORRY FOR THE WAYS I'VE HURT YOU, FATHER. I PRAISE YOU FOR YOUR GOODNESS, YOUR MERCY, AND YOUR LOVE.

Remember Me

Remember this good deed, O my God, and do not forget all that I have faithfully done for the Temple of my God and its services.

NEHEMIAH 13:14 NLT

Nehemiah did a lot to reform the temple. When he found out that some of the workers weren't being paid, he made it right. He worked tirelessly to bring about needed change. We don't have record of anyone thanking him. He probably didn't receive awards or recognition of any kind from other people. Yet that wasn't his goal. His only prayer was that God remember him. He worked to please God and not people.

Many of us have been in the same situation. When you, like Nehemiah, work tirelessly for what is right, without any recognition, remember this. God knows. God sees. And He will not forget.

SOMETIMES I FORGET THAT I LIVE, SERVE, AND WORK FOR YOU, NOT MEN. I DO WHAT'S RIGHT BECAUSE IT HONORS YOU, EVEN WHEN NO ONE NOTICES. THANK YOU FOR REMEMBERING ME, FATHER.

Praise Anyway

At this, Job got up and tore his robe and shaved his head. Then he fell to the ground in worship and said: "Naked I came from my mother's womb, and naked I will depart. The LORD gave and the LORD has taken away; may the name of the LORD be praised." In all this, Job did not sin by charging God with wrongdoing.

JOB 1:20–22 NIV

Job was a wealthy, successful man. Within a few minutes, he lost his livestock, his servants, his property, and all his children. He was in shock. He was utterly broken. In his despair, he cried, tore his clothes, and shaved his head. But he didn't blame God. Instead, he acknowledged that he'd been blessed by God and that it was God's right to take it away. He had no idea that these trials came, not as punishment, but because of God's confidence in Job's reaction.

We all face trials. Like Job, can we praise Him as much in the storm as in the sunlight?

I'M BROKEN, LORD.
BUT I PRAISE YOU ANYWAY.

Keep Talking

"My days are swifter than a runner; they fly away without a glimpse of joy. They skim past like boats of papyrus, like eagles swooping down on their prey. If I say, 'I will forget my complaint, I will change my expression, and smile,' I still dread all my sufferings, for I know you will not hold me innocent."

JOB 9:25–28 NIV

To say Job was depressed is an understatement. He'd lost his family. His land. And his fortune. His "friends" accused him, saying he must have made God mad for all this to happen. His wife was disgusted by his bad breath. On top of it all, he knew his place before God. He knew that even the best of men are guilty of sin. We deserve nothing from Him.

Job felt hopeless, but he never turned against God. He kept talking to his Creator. When things look hopeless to you, keep talking. Keep praying. God hears, and He has good things in store.

I'M IN ANGUISH, LORD. I DON'T KNOW WHAT TO PRAY. BUT I'M HERE.

Listen Up!

Then Job answered the Lord*: "I am unworthy—how can I reply to you? I put my hand over my mouth. I spoke once, but I have no answer—twice, but I will say no more."*

Job 40:3–5 niv

When we think of prayer, we usually think about talking to God. But prayer is more of a conversation. If you speak with someone who does all the talking but doesn't listen to what you have to say, is it really conversing? Job had said his piece. He understood the process. Now it was *his turn to listen.*

When you pray, don't forget to include listening time. Sometimes that can mean studying God's Word, the Bible. Other times, listening means simply being quiet and letting the Holy Spirit reveal things to you.

I'M SORRY FOR DOING ALL THE TALKING IN OUR CONVERSATIONS, LORD. I WANT TO KNOW YOUR THOUGHTS. I NEED TO HEAR YOUR WORDS, YOUR WISDOM, YOUR GUIDANCE. THANK YOU FOR ALWAYS LISTENING TO ME. HELP ME BE A BETTER LISTENER.

Help Me Sleep

I cried aloud to the Lord, and he answered me from his holy hill. I lay down and slept; I woke again, for the Lord sustained me. I will not be afraid of many thousands of people who have set themselves against me all around.

Psalm 3:4–6 ESV

Studies show that anxiety is at an all-time high in our society. Dangerous diseases, political unrest, and cultural wars can cause even the most confident of people to tense up. David wrote this prayer when he fled from his son Absalom, who was trying to usurp the throne. He didn't want to fight his son, because he didn't want to be put in a position to kill him. Talk about stress!

In those anxious moments, David cried out to God, and God answered. He gave David peace and helped him sleep. The same God who helped David through that crisis will help you, as well.

YOU KNOW WHAT I FACE, FATHER.
I'M ANXIOUS AND I CAN'T SLEEP.
GUIDE ME. HELP ME. GIVE ME YOUR PEACE.

Joy and Peace

There are many who say, "Who will show us some good? Lift up the light of your face upon us, O Lord!" You have put more joy in my heart than they have when their grain and wine abound. In peace I will both lie down and sleep; for you alone, O Lord, make me dwell in safety.

Psalm 4:6–8 ESV

The first part of this scripture refers to people who mock God as if He can't *really* do anything. David contradicted their mocking, because he knew the joy that a right relationship with God brings. That joy surpasses the most lavish party! He concluded by praising God for the peace and the confidence that come from knowing He's always watching over us. We can let our guards down. We can relax, rest, and even sleep, knowing God will take care of those who love Him.

TRUSTING YOU ISN'T ALWAYS A POPULAR CHOICE IN OUR SOCIETY, LORD. BUT IT DOESN'T MATTER WHAT OTHERS THINK. I KNOW YOU WILL TAKE CARE OF ME. I LOVE YOU AND TRUST YOU COMPLETELY.

High Regard

But let all who take refuge in you rejoice; let them ever sing for joy, and spread your protection over them, that those who love your name may exult in you. For you bless the righteous, O Lord; you cover him with favor as with a shield.

Psalm 5:11–12 ESV

David knew that God holds in high regard those who love Him. He protects them, blesses them, and guides them. He wraps His presence around them like a shield. These are great verses to use as a prayer for those you love. Ask God to draw them to Himself. Beg Him to turn their hearts to Him, because you know the benefits of a close relationship with God. He always hears our prayers. . .and He loves your friends and family even more than you do.

FATHER, LET THE PEOPLE I CARE ABOUT TAKE REFUGE IN YOU. LET THEM REJOICE IN YOUR PRESENCE. PROTECT THEM, AND COVER THEM LIKE A SHIELD. I KNOW YOU BLESS THE RIGHTEOUS . . .MAKE THEM RIGHTEOUS, LORD.

God holds in
high regard those
who love Him.

In Awe

When I look at your heavens, the work of your fingers, the moon and the stars, which you have set in place, what is man that you are mindful of him, and the son of man that you care for him? Yet you have made him a little lower than the heavenly beings and crowned him with glory and honor.

Psalm 8:3–5 ESV

Too often, we reserve prayer for times when we need something from God. If we're not careful, we can treat prayer like a never-ending wish list. God wants to hear our dreams, our desires, and our needs. But He also longs for our praise. When we pray, it's important to reserve time to just be in awe of God. The fact that He is God, yet He loves *us*, is pretty incredible. Have you told Him that recently?

THANK YOU FOR SHOWING AN INTEREST IN MY LIFE, FATHER. I CAN'T COMPREHEND THAT KIND OF LOVE, BUT I'M SO GRATEFUL FOR IT. I'M IN AWE OF YOU.

Spread the Word

I will give thanks to the LORD with my whole heart; I will recount all of your wonderful deeds. I will be glad and exult in you; I will sing praise to your name, O Most High.

PSALM 9:1–2 ESV

In this passage, David promised God that he would tell everyone about all the great things God has done. He made good on his promise by writing so many of the psalms. Now, thousands of years later, we're still reading them. David also promised to sing praises. We know David was a musician and often sang and played his harp for the Lord where others could hear.

God loves it when we share His love with others. Whether through telling our stories, writing a blog, or singing out, we need to follow David's example. God is good! Spread the word.

YOU'VE BEEN SO KIND TO ME, FATHER! THE STORIES OF YOUR GOODNESS IN MY LIFE NEVER END. LIKE DAVID, I WANT TO THANK YOU, PRAISE YOU, AND TELL EVERYONE I KNOW ABOUT YOUR LOVE.

Where Are You?

Why, O L*ORD*, *do you stand far away?*
Why do you hide yourself in times of trouble?
PSALM 10:1 ESV

God is good, all the time. But we still live in a messed-up world. Sin's effects can make living here difficult. In those hard times, it's okay to question God. He's not offended by our honest feelings—He wants us to talk to Him about whatever's on our minds.

But just because we can't feel His presence doesn't mean He's absent. He's never far away from those who love Him. He is always, always working on our behalf. He doesn't always respond on our desired timeline, but that doesn't mean He's not busy. When He feels far away, trust His goodness, His kindness, and His love.

WHERE ARE YOU, LORD? YOU PROMISED NEVER TO LEAVE ME OR FORSAKE ME, BUT RIGHT NOW, I FEEL ALONE AND FORSAKEN. PLEASE REMIND ME OF YOUR PRESENCE. LET ME SEE YOU WORKING. I LOVE YOU, I TRUST YOU, AND I KNOW YOU ARE GOOD.

We Get Lifted Up

How long, O Lord? Will you forget me forever? How long will you hide your face from me? How long must I take counsel in my soul and have sorrow in my heart all the day? . . . But I have trusted in your steadfast love; my heart shall rejoice in your salvation.

Psalm 13:1–2, 5 ESV

David struggled with depression. He knew that tangible, hard-to-describe feeling of sadness. Yet time and again, we see David begin his prayers with a heavy heart and end them with praise. That's one of the beautiful side effects of worship! When we lift up God, we get lifted up as well.

Next time you're down, follow David's example. Pour out your heart to God. Sit with Him awhile. Let Him wrap His arms around you, and see if you don't feel lifted.

I NEED THE LOVE, COMFORT, AND JOY THAT ONLY COME FROM YOU, FATHER. THANK YOU FOR CARING ABOUT WHAT I'M GOING THROUGH AND FOR GIVING ME THE STRENGTH TO CARRY ON. I PRAISE YOU!

Question and Answer

O Lord, who shall sojourn in your tent? Who shall dwell on your holy hill? He who walks blamelessly and does what is right and speaks truth in his heart; who does not slander with his tongue and does no evil to his neighbor, nor takes up a reproach against his friend; in whose eyes a vile person is despised, but who honors those who fear the Lord; who swears to his own hurt and does not change; who does not put out his money at interest and does not take a bribe against the innocent. He who does these things shall never be moved.

Psalm 15 ESV

In verse 1 of this passage, David asked God who will be allowed into His presence. In verses 2–5, David answered his own question as the Holy Spirit revealed it to him. In summary, the righteous, godly person who loves God with all their heart and hates evil will live with God forever.

THANK YOU FOR YOUR HOLY SPIRIT, WHO GIVES ME WISDOM AND ANSWERS MY QUESTIONS.

In His Presence

You make known to me the path of life; in your presence there is fullness of joy; at your right hand are pleasures forevermore.

Psalm 16:11 ESV

When we read verses like this out of context, it seems like David led an easy, pleasant life. As king, he certainly had pleasure at his fingertips. But we also know that David had plenty of heartache and sorrow. How could David talk about "fullness of joy" and "pleasures forevermore"?

David knew that joy isn't based on our circumstances. It's based on confidence in our future. Earthly pleasure lasts a short time, but God's pleasures last for eternity. Next time you find yourself wondering where the joy is, remind yourself of David's words. We find joy in God's presence. We find pleasure when we're holding His hand. The good life exists wherever our Father is. Stay close to Him, and you'll find these things.

I'M SORRY FOR LOOKING FOR JOY, PEACE, AND PLEASURE IN THE WRONG PLACES. I WANT TO STAY CLOSE TO YOU, FATHER. KEEP ME IN YOUR PRESENCE.

Words and Thoughts

Let the words of my mouth and the meditation of my heart be acceptable in your sight, O Lord, my rock and my redeemer.

Psalm 19:14 ESV

If David and James (from the New Testament) had known each other, they might have had a lively debate about our words. James 3:8 tells us that no one can tame their tongue and that it's full of evil and deadly poison. Those are some pretty strong words! Yet David asked God to make his words and thoughts pleasing to God. So which one is right?

They both are. On our own, we will always say and think things that hurt others, offend God, and harm ourselves. This world is too full of negative influences. Plus, we're ruled by a sinful nature. But with God all things are possible (Matthew 19:26)! Ask God to tame your mind and your tongue and to guide your words and thoughts to be pleasing to Him.

HELP ME, LORD. I WANT MY WORDS AND THOUGHTS TO PLEASE YOU.

Unclean Lips

And I said: "Woe is me! For I am lost; for I am a man of unclean lips, and I dwell in the midst of a people of unclean lips; for my eyes have seen the King, the LORD of hosts!"

ISAIAH 6:5 ESV

In this passage, Isaiah had a vision of himself in the presence of God. He heard the seraphim offer pure praise to their Maker, and Isaiah realized how unclean he was. He knew our words are a reflection of our hearts (Matthew 12:34). We can try to change our speaking patterns, but if our hearts aren't changed, we'll fall back into the same patterns of gossip, slander, and negative talk. While we can't control every thought that enters our minds, we can control which ones we dwell on. Choose to meditate on praise, and watch your speech become more pleasing to God.

MY THOUGHTS CAN BE MEAN, JUDGMENTAL, AND SINFUL, LORD. BUT I WANT TO PLEASE YOU. HELP ME FOCUS ON YOUR GOODNESS, AND LET MY WORDS REFLECT YOUR PRAISE.

Mocking God

"Incline your ear, O Lord, and hear; open your eyes, O Lord, and see; and hear all the words of Sennacherib, which he has sent to mock the living God."
Isaiah 37:17 ESV

Sennacherib was the king of the Assyrians. He invaded Judah and mocked God every chance he got. Hezekiah, king of Judah, was a godly king, and it broke his heart to hear God mocked. He begged God to show His power so the mocking would stop.

In our culture, God is often mocked. It's become so commonplace that many Christians aren't even affected. When someone makes fun of God or His Word or uses His name in a disrespectful way, what is your response? Does your spirit feel assaulted, or do you even notice? Ask God to make your heart sensitive to insults to His character. Ask Him to show Himself so the mocking will stop.

I'M SORRY FOR BRUSHING IT OFF
WHEN OTHERS INSULT YOU, LORD.
TEACH ME TO RESPOND WITH WISDOM.
SHOW YOUR POWER SO PEOPLE
WILL LOVE AND RESPECT YOU.

Hope in the Lord

Let your steadfast love, O Lord,
be upon us, even as we hope in you.
Psalm 33:22 ESV

Do you hope in the Lord, or is your default setting stuck in a negative loop? Hope is the opposite of fear and anxiety. Hope is the belief that good things are in store, while fear is the belief that something bad will happen. Although fear and anxiety are normal emotions that everyone has, they should never become our permanent address. God's promises are true and unchanging, and He promises good to those who love Him. When you're going through a difficult time, focus on God's love and the joyful future He has in store for you.

MY HEART OFTEN SITS IN ANXIETY, FATHER. IT'S COMFORTABLE WITH FEAR, ANGER, AND OTHER NEGATIVE EMOTIONS. I WANT MY DEFAULT SETTING TO BE HOPE, BUT I NEED YOUR HELP. I WANT TO FOCUS ON ALL THE GOOD THINGS YOU HAVE IN STORE FOR MY LIFE. SHOW ME YOUR POWER. LET ME FEEL YOUR PRESENCE. I WANT TO LIVE IN YOUR LOVE.

God's calling doesn't
require self-confidence
as much as
God-confidence.

God-fidence

Now the word of the Lord came to me, saying, "Before I formed you in the womb I knew you, and before you were born I consecrated you; I appointed you a prophet to the nations." Then I said, "Ah, Lord God! Behold, I do not know how to speak, for I am only a youth."

Jeremiah 1:4–6 esv

Isn't it just like a teenager to argue with the Almighty? Young people will often argue with anyone. Jeremiah heard God Himself tell him, "This is what I made you for." But Jeremiah lacked self-confidence.

Many of us are guilty of the same thing. We don't think we have what it takes to serve God, so we question our calling. We say, "If I try to tell others about You, I'll mess it up. I'll offend someone. I might even lose my job." But God's calling doesn't require *self-confidence* as much as *God-confidence*. It's okay to tell God your fears, but in the end, trust Him. He made you for this.

I WANT TO FULFILL YOUR CALLING ON MY LIFE.

About Time

"O Lord, make me know my end and what is the measure of my days; let me know how fleeting I am! Behold, you have made my days a few handbreadths, and my lifetime is as nothing before you. Surely all mankind stands as a mere breath! Surely a man goes about as a shadow! Surely for nothing they are in turmoil; man heaps up wealth and does not know who will gather!"

Psalm 39:4–6 ESV

David's thoughts apply to our most persistent anxieties. Why do we worry about wealth, success, and status? What does it matter, really? We are but a wisp in time. When we're looking to the future, it seems to stretch out endlessly. When we go through difficult times, they seem to go on forever. But most adults will agree that when they look back at their lives, time has evaporated like a mist. Decades seem like moments. Don't waste a minute worrying about things that God's already taken care of.

REMIND ME OF WHAT'S IMPORTANT, LORD. I DON'T WANT TO WASTE MY TIME HERE.

When You Don't Understand

Righteous are you, O Lord, when I complain to you; yet I would plead my case before you. Why does the way of the wicked prosper? Why do all who are treacherous thrive?

Jeremiah 12:1 ESV

Is it okay to complain to God? The answer is yes, as long as we recognize God's complete and total righteousness. Jeremiah's complaint here wasn't an accusation. Instead, he simply wanted to understand. It didn't make sense to him that he, God's chosen prophet, should suffer so much when the wicked seemed to be prospering.

Sometimes, the Holy Spirit gives us understanding. But even when He doesn't, we can still trust that God's ways are higher than our ways (Isaiah 55:8–9). He is only good, and all His actions are born of love and a desire for justice. One day, we'll see the bigger picture. Until then, we just need to trust Him.

THANK YOU FOR LISTENING TO MY QUESTIONS AND COMPLAINTS, FATHER. I KNOW YOU ARE GOOD, AND I TRUST YOU, EVEN WHEN THINGS DON'T MAKE SENSE.

Plea for Mercy

We acknowledge our wickedness, O Lord, and the iniquity of our fathers, for we have sinned against you. Do not spurn us, for your name's sake; do not dishonor your glorious throne; remember and do not break your covenant with us.

Jeremiah 14:20–21 ESV

In this prayer, Jeremiah admitted to the sins the Israelites had committed. They were guilty, and they deserved punishment. But Jeremiah begged for mercy. He reminded God of His promises, of His covenant relationship.

No matter what we've done, we can always come to God, admit our guilt, and ask for mercy. Sometimes, He will withhold the punishment we deserve here on earth. Other times, we'll have to deal with the consequences of our actions. But we can be sure that everyone with a truly repentant heart who accepts Christ's salvation will receive mercy, kindness, compassion, and love when we one day stand before God.

I'VE REALLY MESSED UP, LORD.
I WAS WRONG, AND I'M SO SORRY.
PLEASE SHOW MERCY ON ME, AND GIVE
ME THE STRENGTH TO DEAL WITH THE
CONSEQUENCES OF MY ACTIONS.

From the Pit

"I called on your name, O Lord, from the depths of the pit;
you heard my plea, 'Do not close your ear to my cry for help!'"
Lamentations 3:55–56 ESV

The book of Lamentations was written by the prophet Jeremiah. It's a record of his sorrow and broken heart over the destruction of Jerusalem and the temple. His words are raw. . .he was calling out from his gut, from the deepest, lowest point of pain he experienced.

We've all been in that pit at some point. When we're at the bottom, and the only place to look is up, we can be certain our Father is right there with us. Call out to Him—He's listening. Wrap your arms around His neck, and let His Spirit absorb your sobs. He knows you're hurting, and He wants to comfort you and give you peace.

I'M HURTING MORE THAN I CAN DESCRIBE, LORD. PLEASE GIVE ME SOME RELIEF. I NEED YOUR COMFORT, YOUR PRESENCE, AND YOUR PEACE.

Thirsty for God

As a deer pants for flowing streams,
so pants my soul for you, O God.
PSALM 42:1 ESV

This beautiful prayer was penned by the sons of Korah. Originally, this family rebelled against Moses during their time in the desert. They were killed for their disobedience to God, but a few of them survived. Their descendants repented, and future generations learned from their ancestors' mistakes. They faithfully served God, eventually becoming gatekeepers for the tabernacle once they arrived in the Promised Land. They served as the choir/praise team for worship.

Micah 6:8 tells us that God loves mercy. He always gives us a second chance. No matter who your family is or what you've done in the past, you can always turn around and run back to Him. He will welcome you back with arms held wide.

I LONG FOR YOU JUST AS THESE MEN WITH A SHADY PAST LONGED FOR YOUR PRESENCE. I THIRST FOR YOU, FATHER. THANK YOU FOR SECOND CHANCES AND FOR ALWAYS WELCOMING ME BACK.

When Relationships Are Hard

Be gracious to me, O God, for man tramples on me; all day long an attacker oppresses me; my enemies trample on me all day long, for many attack me proudly. When I am afraid, I put my trust in you. In God, whose word I praise, in God I trust; I shall not be afraid. What can flesh do to me?

Psalm 56:1–4 ESV

Life is hard. Relationships are hard. Sometimes, it feels like the people who should love and support us most are the ones who wound us the deepest. This kind of betrayal hurts to the core. But God knows what you're going through. He sees it all. And He can redeem any situation, no matter how hopeless it may seem. He can turn anything around for our good and His glory.

When you're hurt and afraid, trust Him. Rest in His love. And remember that He is always, only good.

YOU KNOW HOW OTHERS ARE HURTING ME RIGHT NOW, FATHER. PLEASE REDEEM THIS SITUATION—YOU ARE THE ONLY ONE WHO CAN.

Obey Anyway

I heard what he said, but I did not understand what he meant. So I asked, "How will all this finally end, my lord?"
DANIEL 12:8 NLT

In this verse, Daniel had just seen a vision about the end times. Though he wrote it down, he didn't understand all he'd seen. He asked God to explain.

God answered, "It's not for you to understand. You've done your part. You wrote these things down. You'll just have to trust that others will come along after you to fill in the gaps."

We often see only our part of the puzzle. It would be nice if we could follow every project to completion. We witness to someone and they believe in Jesus. We give money to a cause and it results in amazing things. But most of the time, we don't get to see the end results of our obedience. That's okay. Obey anyway.

I WISH I UNDERSTOOD ALL YOU'RE ASKING ME TO GO THROUGH, LORD. EVEN WHEN I DON'T, I WANT TO OBEY YOU COMPLETELY.

Bragging on God

For not in my bow do I trust, nor can my sword save me. But you have saved us from our foes and have put to shame those who hate us. In God we have boasted continually, and we will give thanks to your name forever.

PSALM 44:6–8 ESV

Don't you love it when someone praises you for a job well done? Most of us stand a little taller when others brag on us. That makes sense, because we're made in God's image. He loves it when we brag on Him! Truly, He is worthy of all the bragging, all the praise we can give Him.

Yet all too often, we give credit to our money or our abilities or something else. We forget that every good gift is from God. He deserves all the recognition for the good things in our lives. Brag on Him, every chance you get!

THANK YOU FOR ALL THE AMAZING THINGS YOU'VE DONE AND CONTINUE TO DO, EVERY SINGLE DAY. GIVE ME OPPORTUNITIES TO BRAG ON YOU!

A Clean Heart

Create in me a clean heart, O God, and renew a right spirit within me. Cast me not away from your presence, and take not your Holy Spirit from me. Restore to me the joy of your salvation, and uphold me with a willing spirit.
PSALM 51:10–12 ESV

David wrote this prayer after he'd committed adultery with Bathsheba, gotten her pregnant, then had her husband killed to cover up his actions. The prophet Nathan confronted David, and shame flooded his being. He knew he'd messed up, and one of his biggest fears was that God would withhold His presence, guidance, and love from David.

Yes, David did some pretty bad things. . .yet he was called "a man after [God's] own heart" (1 Samuel 13:14). How can that be? God knows we'll make mistakes. But when we humbly admit our mistakes, ask for forgiveness, and commit to changing our ways, He forgives us and welcomes us back into His presence.

CREATE IN ME A CLEAN HEART, LORD. RENEW A RIGHT SPIRIT WITHIN ME.

Broken Heart

O Lord, open my lips, and my mouth will declare your praise. For you will not delight in sacrifice, or I would give it; you will not be pleased with a burnt offering. The sacrifices of God are a broken spirit; a broken and contrite heart, O God, you will not despise.

PSALM 51:15–17 ESV

This is a continuation of David's prayer after his adultery and murder were discovered. David knew he couldn't make his actions right with a big donation to the temple or a grand show of piety. God isn't impressed by those things. Instead, God wants us to be truly sorry for our sins. He wants us to *long* to be like Him: godly, humble, compassionate, and righteous.

David showed none of those qualities when he slept with Uriah's wife then had Uriah killed. He was ashamed of his actions, to the point of a broken heart. No matter what we've done, if we're truly sorry and want to change, God is pleased.

I'M SO SORRY FOR THE SINFUL CHOICES I'VE MADE, FATHER. HELP ME CHANGE.

Change My Heart

He prayed to the LORD*, "Isn't this what I said,* LORD*, when I was still at home? That is what I tried to forestall by fleeing to Tarshish. I knew that you are a gracious and compassionate God, slow to anger and abounding in love, a God who relents from sending calamity. Now,* LORD*, take away my life, for it is better for me to die than to live."*

JONAH 4:2–3 NIV

Jonah didn't like Ninevites. They were awful people. So when God sent Jonah to Nineveh to encourage them to repent and turn to Him, Jonah went the other way. After quite a journey (which temporarily landed him in a fish's belly), Jonah obeyed.

Sure enough, the Ninevites repented, and Jonah was mad. He wanted them to be punished, not saved! He pouted and asked God to just let him die. Can't you just see God rolling His eyes? It's hard to accept that God loves the people we can't stand. Ask God to change your heart to reflect His love.

CHANGE MY HEART, LORD.

Ask God to
change your heart
to reflect His love.

Trust His Heart

How long, Lord, must I call for help, but you do not listen? Or cry out to you, "Violence!" but you do not save? Why do you make me look at injustice? Why do you tolerate wrongdoing? Destruction and violence are before me; there is strife, and conflict abounds. Therefore the law is paralyzed, and justice never prevails. The wicked hem in the righteous, so that justice is perverted.

Habakkuk 1:2–4 niv

Like so many prophets before him, Habakkuk issued this complaint against God. When we're frustrated about our circumstances, it's okay to tell God. It's okay to ask Him why. God isn't put off by our honest prayers.

In the next verse, God answered. "Look among the nations, and see; wonder and be astounded. For I am doing a work in your days that you would not believe if told" (verse 5 esv). Even when we can't understand what God is doing, He is always working on our behalf. Trust His power. Trust His love. Trust His heart.

I DON'T UNDERSTAND.
BUT I TRUST YOU, LORD.

Keep It Simple

"And when you pray, do not heap up empty phrases as the Gentiles do, for they think that they will be heard for their many words. Do not be like them, for your Father knows what you need before you ask him."

MATTHEW 6:7–8 ESV

Just before this, Jesus discussed the way hypocrites pray. He said they stand on the street corner and pray loudly so people will be impressed with how spiritual they are. Here He tells us not to use fancy words and phrases. God loves our simple prayers and conversations. He longs for a real, authentic relationship with us. We don't need to impress Him—He already knows everything about us. And we certainly don't need to impress others with our prayers. No one besides God has the power to answer them. When you talk to God, keep it simple. Keep it honest. And keep it real.

I'M SO GLAD I CAN BE REAL WITH YOU, FATHER. YOU KNOW MY HEART-THE GOOD AND THE BAD. I GIVE IT ALL TO YOU.

Teach Me to Pray

"Our Father in heaven, hallowed be your name, your kingdom come, your will be done, on earth as it is in heaven. Give us today our daily bread. And forgive us our debts, as we also have forgiven our debtors. And lead us not into temptation, but deliver us from the evil one."

MATTHEW 6:9–13 NIV

It wasn't Jesus' intention that we pray these exact words. Instead, He gave us an example. One common memory aid for praying this way is *Up, Down, In, Out.* First, pray up—focus on who God is. Praise Him. Worship Him. Next, we come back down to ourselves. We react to His holiness by asking His will to be done on earth—through us. Third, we can move inward and make our requests—*Give us bread*. Finally, we move outward—*Help me avoid temptation.* There are many ways to pray, but the most important thing is to make prayer a regular priority in your life.

TEACH ME TO PRAY. I LONG FOR YOU, LORD.

On Being Holy

"Our Father in heaven, hallowed be your name."
MATTHEW 6:9 NIV

Hallowed is another word for *holy*. The definition of *holy* is "set apart for a higher purpose." We're told in 1 Peter 1:16 that we should be holy because God is holy. As Christians, we're all set apart for a higher purpose. Although we will never attain God's level of holiness here on earth, that should be our goal. To understand that kind of holiness, it's important to meditate on God's character. He is truly holy: sacred, consecrated, dedicated to a higher calling. That calling, for Him, is to love us and bring us into relationship with Him. For us, it's to love others and point them to God.

Think about God's holiness today. How does His purpose impact your own purpose while you're here on earth?

YOU ARE HOLY, FATHER. IT TAKES AWHILE FOR THE MEANING OF THAT WORD TO SINK IN. YOU ARE PERFECT, SACRED, AND CONSECRATED. THANK YOU FOR LOVING SOMEONE LIKE ME. TEACH ME TO BE HOLY TOO.

His Kingdom on Earth

"Your kingdom come."
MATTHEW 6:10 NIV

Three little words. . .yet they hold such power. When Jesus prayed, "Your kingdom come," He was asking God to extend His reign from heaven to earth. He wanted God to stop evil for good. . .to draw every heart to Himself. . .to make His love and character known to all.

One day, His kingdom will come permanently. In the meantime, God invites us to help extend His reign here. We are His hands and feet on earth. It's our job to promote justice and righteousness. When we live out His purpose, He uses us to help stop evil, share His love, and draw others to His character by showing His goodness, kindness, mercy, and compassion.

Right here, right now, God's reign on earth is up to us. Our actions bring His kingdom here.

I WANT YOUR KINGDOM TO RULE HERE ON EARTH, LORD. LET IT BEGIN WITH ME. FILL ME WITH YOUR LOVE. WHEN OTHERS LOOK AT ME, LET THEM SEE YOU.

God's Will on Earth

"Your will be done, on earth as it is in heaven."
MATTHEW 6:10 NIV

Is God's will always done here on earth? Nothing happens without God's permission. But God gives us a lot of freedom. He didn't create us to be robots, doing His will because we have no choice. That freedom means many people will habitually choose sin. Sin deforms this world and degrades our lives.

So the answer is no; God's will isn't always done. He wants us to choose Him and His ways, and not everyone does. When we pray for His will to be done on earth as it is in heaven, we pray for people to choose Him. We pray for the world to operate according to His original plan. The best way for that to happen is to start by praying for His will to be done in our own lives and in the lives of those around us.

FATHER, PLEASE ACCOMPLISH YOUR WILL HERE, NOW, TODAY, IN MY LIFE AND IN ALL THOSE I LOVE.

Daily Bread

"Give us today our daily bread."
MATTHEW 6:11 NIV

According to a recent survey by the American Psychological Association, more than 70 percent of Americans say money is a high source of anxiety. They worry about having enough money, about making more money, about how to spend it and how to save it. God doesn't want us stressing about money. He wants us to trust Him for today.

Next time you feel anxious over whether you can pay your bills or buy groceries, ask yourself, "Do I have what I need right now?" If not, ask God to meet those needs. He has the best connections! You may be surprised at how He provides for you. Ask Him to make you a wise spender and saver. But don't stress! God loves you. He wants to take care of you. And He wants you to trust Him.

YOU KNOW I'M CONCERNED ABOUT MEETING MY NEEDS AND MY FAMILY'S NEEDS. I WILL TRUST YOU TO PROVIDE TODAY. I KNOW YOU'LL TAKE CARE OF TOMORROW TOO.

Forgive Your Debtors

"And forgive us our debts, as we also have forgiven our debtors."
MATTHEW 6:12 NIV

The more someone has wronged us, the harder it can be to let them off the hook. It's important to remember that forgiveness doesn't mean we're saying "It's okay" or "It's no big deal." Instead, it's saying, "What you did is not okay. I condemn your actions, but I care about you as a person. I will not hang on to the pain you caused me. I forgive you."

Forgiveness also doesn't mean forgetting. If you wreck my car, I can forgive you, but I don't have to let you borrow my car again. If you abuse me, I can forgive you, but I can also set boundaries for how much access you have to my life. Forgiveness means we let go of the debt someone owes us. We mark it off our list. Instead of stressing about it, we can walk away, leave it behind, and get on with our lives.

THANK YOU FOR FORGIVING ME.
HELP ME FORGIVE OTHERS.

Avoiding Temptation

"And lead us not into temptation, but deliver us from the evil one."
MATTHEW 6:13 NIV

Temptation holds a different form for each person. Some of us tend toward alcoholism or substance abuse. Others aren't tempted by those things at all, but they are the first to listen to and spread gossip. Whether it's binge eating, lying, or sexual sin, Satan knows your weakness. He's a master strategist, and he will absolutely make it as hard as possible for you to avoid your downfall.

That's why we must rely on God's help to keep us pure. If we stay close to Him, He will lead us away from temptation, away from evil, and keep us safe from sin. Ask Him today and every day to protect you and your loved ones from Satan's traps.

I CAN'T DO THIS ALONE, FATHER.
I'M NOT STRONG ENOUGH. . .
MY WILLPOWER ISN'T POWERFUL
ENOUGH. I NEED YOUR STRENGTH IN ME.
STEER ME AWAY FROM TEMPTATION AND
PROTECT ME FROM SATAN. EVEN WHEN
I PULL AWAY, KEEP ME CLOSE TO YOU.

A Soldier's Faith

"Lord," he said, "my servant lies at home paralyzed, suffering terribly." Jesus said to him, "Shall I come and heal him?" The centurion replied, "Lord, I do not deserve to have you come under my roof. But just say the word, and my servant will be healed. For I myself am a man under authority, with soldiers under me. I tell this one, 'Go,' and he goes; and that one, 'Come,' and he comes. I say to my servant, 'Do this,' and he does it."

MATTHEW 8:6–9 NIV

Jesus must have had to stop a moment and add up the pieces to this puzzle. Christ's own people, who had been brought up to know and trust God's Word, lacked faith. But this centurion—a Roman soldier—had no trouble believing that Jesus was who He said He was. He knew that Jesus had the power to control sickness and disease and weather and demons. . .this man knew that everything in creation submitted to Jesus' command.

Do you have that kind of faith?

YOU ARE ALL-POWERFUL.
YOU CAN DO ANYTHING. I TRUST YOU.

Where's Your Faith?

The disciples went and woke him, saying, "Lord, save us! We're going to drown!" He replied, "You of little faith, why are you so afraid?" Then he got up and rebuked the winds and the waves, and it was completely calm.

MATTHEW 8:25–26 NIV

Do you ever wonder if Jesus got frustrated with His disciples at times? He must have. After all they'd seen, after all the people He'd healed and the miracles He'd performed, they still worried about a storm. Many of us can look back at our own lives and recount time and again when God took care of us. Yet the moment another storm hits the horizon, we freak out. We panic and worry and wring our hands and bite our nails and beg God to do something. He must look at us the same way Jesus looked at His friends and say, "You of little faith. Why are you so afraid?"

I TRUST YOU, FATHER, BUT MY FAITH IS STILL GROWING. THANK YOU FOR YOUR PATIENCE WITH ME. I KNOW YOU'LL ALWAYS TAKE CARE OF ME.

When Demons Prayed

"What do you want with us, Son of God?" they shouted. "Have you come here to torture us before the appointed time?" Some distance from them a large herd of pigs was feeding. The demons begged Jesus, "If you drive us out, send us into the herd of pigs."

MATTHEW 8:29–31 NIV

When we think of prayer, we don't often picture demons. Yet that's what happened in this story. . .the demons prayed! They knew the extent of God's power. They didn't want to be sent back to hell—they knew firsthand how awful that place is. It's funny that demons asked God for mercy. . .and He showed it. He cast them into a pig herd instead of back to hell.

If demons know how powerful prayer is, why do we ever doubt its effectiveness? When we pray, we address the almighty God. And unlike those demons, God loves us.

THANK YOU FOR ALWAYS LISTENING TO ME, FATHER. WHAT A PRIVILEGE IT IS FOR ME TO TALK TO YOU ANYTIME I WANT.

People may laugh
at our faith.
But hope placed in
God is never misspent.

Hope in God

While he was saying this, a synagogue leader came and knelt before him and said, "My daughter has just died. But come and put your hand on her, and she will live." . . . When Jesus entered the synagogue leader's house and saw the noisy crowd and people playing pipes, he said, "Go away. The girl is not dead but asleep." But they laughed at him. After the crowd had been put outside, he went in and took the girl by the hand, and she got up.

MATTHEW 9:18, 23–25 NIV

There's perhaps nothing more devastating than losing a child. That's not the natural order of things. This synagogue leader watched his precious daughter die, and he'd heard that Jesus could heal the sick. Maybe He could bring his little girl back to life! His faith was greater than the mourners at his house. When Jesus said the girl was only sleeping, they laughed.

People may laugh at our faith. But hope placed in God is never misspent.

I NEED A MIRACLE, LORD.
YOU ARE MY HOPE.

Touching His Cloak

Just then a woman who had been subject to bleeding for twelve years came up behind him and touched the edge of his cloak. She said to herself, "If I only touch his cloak, I will be healed." Jesus turned and saw her. "Take heart, daughter," he said, "your faith has healed you." And the woman was healed at that moment.

MATTHEW 9:20–22 NIV

Do you wonder how Jesus knew that this woman had touched His garment? There was a lot going on. Many people were around. An important man had just asked Jesus to heal his daughter. In the midst of it all, Jesus stopped and looked around. Did He feel the power leave Him? Did He sense her presence? She hadn't spoken to Him. . .only to herself.

Her faith moved Him, and she was healed instantly. Our pure, focused belief in His power moves Him as well. When we truly believe, He stops. He looks at us. And He responds to our faith.

I NEED YOUR TOUCH, FATHER.
I KNOW YOU CAN MEET MY NEED.

Walking on Water

"Lord, if it's you," Peter replied,
"tell me to come to you on the water."
MATTHEW 14:28 NIV

Peter often gets a bad rap. If you read the end of the story, you know that Peter got out of the boat, walked on the water with Jesus, then got scared. When his fear took over, he started to sink. We often recall Peter's lack of faith. . .but remember, he was the only one who got out of the boat. He was the only one who had enough faith to step onto the water.

Jesus knows we're human. He knows we'll struggle with fear and anxiety and distractions. Still, He holds out His hand and says, "Come." Yes, we will mess up. We may sink. But when we step out in faith, we'll experience more of His power than those who stay in the safety zone. What will it take for you to step out of your boat and walk with Him?

I WANT TO WALK ON WATER
WITH YOU, JESUS.

Getting Distracted

But when he saw the wind, he was afraid and, beginning to sink, cried out, "Lord, save me!"
MATTHEW 14:30 NIV

Peter was the only one with enough faith to get out of the boat and walk on water. But even after experiencing the power that accompanies that kind of faith, he wavered. He got distracted. And when his faith was replaced by fear, he started to sink. Even then, he called out to Jesus to save him.

We do the same thing. We have moments of great faith, and we're caught up in God's power. But then life comes along and blows fierce winds our direction, and we get distracted. We let go of God's power and let fear take over. It happens to the best of us. Our lack of faith doesn't change God's love for us. No matter what, we can always call out for Him to save us. Reach out your hand. He's right there.

I'M SORRY FOR GETTING DISTRACTED AND LETTING FEAR TAKE OVER. PLEASE SAVE ME! YOU'RE THE ONLY ONE WHO CAN.

Great Faith

A Canaanite woman from that vicinity came to him, crying out, "Lord, Son of David, have mercy on me! My daughter is demon-possessed and suffering terribly." . . . He answered, "I was sent only to the lost sheep of Israel." The woman came and knelt before him. "Lord, help me!" she said. He replied, "It is not right to take the children's bread and toss it to the dogs." "Yes it is, Lord," she said. "Even the dogs eat the crumbs that fall from their master's table."

MATTHEW 15:22, 24–27 NIV

To some, this passage seems disrespectful. Why would Jesus call this woman a dog? Yet Jesus had a purpose for this conversation. She was a Gentile, yet she knew He was the Messiah. He used the *Gentile* word for dog, which meant "pet." She wasn't a member of the family. . .but was still viewed with affection. In verse 28, He said her faith was great and healed her daughter instantly. No matter who we are, God responds to our faith.

HELP ME, LORD.
YOU'RE THE ONLY ONE WHO CAN.

A Bold Request

"What is it you want?" he asked. She said,
"Grant that one of these two sons of mine may sit at
your right and the other at your left in your kingdom."
MATTHEW 20:21 NIV

There are few things a mother won't do for her children. This woman's sons, James and John, were Jesus' disciples. She knew that Jesus was God's son, and she was proud that He'd chosen her boys to be in His inner circle. To sit at His right and left meant to be numbers two and three in the kingdom.

Jesus replied that it wasn't His choice. God would choose who would sit where. Understandably, the other disciples still got upset. Who did this woman think she was? Why did she think her sons were better than the rest of them?

This is one reason why humility is so important to God. When we give ourselves more importance than we give others, we cause friction, relationships suffer, and everyone is miserable.

SHOW ME WHAT IT MEANS TO BE HUMBLE.

Power in Numbers

Two blind men were sitting by the roadside, and when they heard that Jesus was going by, they shouted, "Lord, Son of David, have mercy on us!" The crowd rebuked them and told them to be quiet, but they shouted all the louder, "Lord, Son of David, have mercy on us!" Jesus stopped and called them. "What do you want me to do for you?" he asked. "Lord," they answered, "we want our sight."

MATTHEW 20:30–33 NIV

These two blind guys somehow found each other. They were outcasts, but even outcasts do okay if they have a friend. These fellows had heard about Jesus and decided to do whatever it took to get His attention. Together, they yelled as loud as they could. When people told them to be quiet, they yelled louder. If there had been only one of them, their courage may have waned.

Christian friends are important. Commit to pray for your friends, and share your prayer needs with them as well. There is power in numbers!

SEND ME CHRISTIAN FRIENDS, LORD.

Human Nature

And going a little farther he fell on his face and prayed, saying, "My Father, if it be possible, let this cup pass from me; nevertheless, not as I will, but as you will."
MATTHEW 26:39 ESV

Jesus wouldn't have been human if He'd been fine with what He knew was coming. He didn't say, "Oh, you're gonna whip Me until I bleed, strip Me naked and pound nails into My hands and feet. . .you're gonna spit on Me and call Me names and jam some nasty, deep thorns into My skull. . .sure. Sounds fun." No normal, fully functioning person would welcome the kind of pain and humiliation Jesus knew was coming.

It's okay to tell God that we don't want to do something or face what's coming. Those kinds of emotions are part of what make us human. But like Christ, we must be willing to say, "Not my will, but Yours."

I DON'T WANT TO FACE THIS, LORD. PLEASE KEEP ME FROM HAVING TO DO THIS. BUT I'LL DO WHATEVER YOU SAY. I TRUST YOU.

Feels like Forsaken

And about the ninth hour Jesus cried out with a loud voice, saying, "Eli, Eli, lema sabachthani?" that is, "My God, my God, why have you forsaken me?"
MATTHEW 27:46 ESV

Do you ever feel like God's forsaken you? He promised never to leave us or turn His back on us, but it doesn't always feel that way. In our darkest moments, we may call out the same words that Christ uttered on the cross. *Why have You forsaken me?*

The answer is He hasn't. He loves us. He knows what we're going through, and He hates the pain we feel. But with us, just as with Christ, He has a plan. All things aren't good, but He will weave it all together to make something beautiful. Our experiences, both good and bad, both joyful and pain filled, make us who we are. And that unique perspective makes us better able to live out our divine purpose here on earth.

I KNOW YOU PROMISED NEVER TO FORSAKE ME, BUT THIS SURE FEELS LIKE FORSAKEN, LORD. REMIND ME OF YOUR LOVE.

Because He Loves Me

"Because he loves me," says the L*ORD*, *"I will rescue him; I will protect him, for he acknowledges my name. He will call on me, and I will answer him; I will be with him in trouble, I will deliver him and honor him. With long life I will satisfy him and show him my salvation."*

PSALM 91:14–16 NIV

This passage is one of those *wow* sections of the Bible that we need to hold close every day of our lives. In these verses, God is talking. He says He'll protect us, rescue us, answer us, stay with us through hard times, deliver us out of trouble, set us in a place of honor, and give us a long, satisfying life. That's a lot of promises. And the only thing we have to do to cash in on these promises is love Him.

We don't have to be perfect. We don't have to jump through hoops. He sees our hearts, and it makes Him *so happy* when we sincerely love Him.

I LOVE YOU, FATHER.

Righteous and Devout

"Lord, now you are letting your servant depart in peace, according to your word; for my eyes have seen your salvation that you have prepared in the presence of all peoples, a light for revelation to the Gentiles, and for glory to your people Israel."

LUKE 2:29–32 ESV

These words were spoken by Simeon. The Bible tells us he was righteous and devout. The Holy Spirit revealed to him that before he died, he'd see the promised Messiah. On that day, Simeon felt prompted by the Holy Spirit to go to the temple, and guess who was there. Mary and Joseph, with their infant son, Jesus. Simeon knew immediately who this was, and he rejoiced and praised God.

God *loves* it when we love Him. He has so many wonderful things in store, in this life as well as in eternity, for those who are righteous and devout. What amazing thing might He have in store for you?

HELP ME BE RIGHTEOUS AND DEVOUT. THANK YOU FOR THE WONDERFUL THINGS YOU HAVE IN STORE FOR MY LIFE.

What we do with
our money is a
reflection of our
relationship with God.

Money Talks

"And he called out, 'Father Abraham, have mercy on me, and send Lazarus to dip the end of his finger in water and cool my tongue, for I am in anguish in this flame.' But Abraham said, 'Child, remember that you in your lifetime received your good things, and Lazarus in like manner bad things; but now he is comforted here, and you are in anguish.'"

LUKE 16:24–25 ESV

In this passage, Jesus tells of a rich man who, in life, didn't care enough about a poor man (Lazarus) to walk to his gate and give him food. Now he wants Lazarus to leave heaven, come to Hades, and give him some water. Even in the afterlife, he treats Lazarus like a servant to do his bidding. He really doesn't get it.

There's much to learn from this story, but one of the simplest themes is this: What we do with our money is a reflection of our relationship with God. God blesses us so we can bless others.

TEACH ME TO BLESS OTHERS WITH MY MONEY.

Before It's Too Late

"And he said, 'Then I beg you, father, to send him to my father's house—for I have five brothers—so that he may warn them, lest they also come into this place of torment.' But Abraham said, 'They have Moses and the Prophets; let them hear them.'"

LUKE 16:27–29 ESV

This passage continues Jesus' story of the rich man in hell. The fact that he's praying to Abraham and not God shows he was *religious*. . .but religion doesn't guarantee salvation. Once he realizes that it's too late to change anything for himself, he wants Lazarus to go back and warn his family members. But just as the man was given plenty of chances with God while he was alive, his brothers would have chances to choose for themselves, as well.

Is God speaking to your heart? Respond now. Come to Him. Embrace Him. Share that love with all who are important to you. One day, it will be too late.

HELP ME MAKE THE MOST OF MY TIME HERE, TO LOVE YOU AND OTHERS.

Stop Comparing

"Two men went up into the temple to pray, one a Pharisee and the other a tax collector. The Pharisee, standing by himself, prayed thus: 'God, I thank you that I am not like other men, extortioners, unjust, adulterers, or even like this tax collector. I fast twice a week; I give tithes of all that I get.'"

LUKE 18:10–12 ESV

In Jewish culture, Pharisees were admired for their high morality, while tax collectors were despised for cheating people. But God looks at things differently than we do. While we see the outside, the obvious, the picture-perfect social media life, God sees our hearts. It seems this Pharisee was more concerned about *looking good* than about *being good*. He was more focused on being *better* than on being *righteous*.

It's normal for others' opinions to matter to us. But it's far more important what God thinks of us.

I'M SORRY FOR THINKING I'M BETTER THAN OTHERS. I'M SORRY FOR ALL THE THINGS I'VE DONE TO DISAPPOINT YOU. I WANT TO PLEASE YOU AND LOVE OTHERS.

Be Humble

"But the tax collector, standing far off, would not even lift up his eyes to heaven, but beat his breast, saying, 'God, be merciful to me, a sinner!' I tell you, this man went down to his house justified, rather than the other. For everyone who exalts himself will be humbled, but the one who humbles himself will be exalted."

Luke 18:13–14 ESV

This story is filled with comparisons. The Pharisee (see verses 11–12) compares himself with the tax collector, and Jesus compared those two as well. It seems both men get what they want when they pray. The Pharisee prays loudly, in public, because he wants attention and admiration from others. The tax collector wants forgiveness. The Pharisee exalts himself, but Jesus said that one day he'll be humbled. The tax collector knows how bad he is. He humbly asks for God's mercy, and he will receive it and so much more.

BEING HUMBLE IS A HARD, ONGOING LESSON, LORD. I'M SORRY FOR MY PRIDE AND FOR THINKING I'M BETTER THAN OTHERS. HAVE MERCY ON ME, A SINNER.

Forgive Them

Jesus said, "Father, forgive them, for they know not what they do." And they cast lots to divide his garments.

LUKE 23:34 ESV

Today, in the United States, the death penalty is controversial. Even in states where the death penalty is an option, it's viewed with a solemn attitude. The convicted person gets to choose their last meal. During the execution, people in the room are quiet and respectful. But that didn't happen with Christ. He suffered countless indignities, including being stripped and beaten in front of an audience. He was mocked and spit on. They put a snarky sign above His head that read KING OF THE JEWS, and they crowned Him with a wreath of long, brutal thorns jammed into His skull. As if that weren't enough, they gambled for His clothes, right at His feet as He hung dying.

And yet, He asked God to forgive them. He knew they didn't understand the gravity of what they did. When people hurt us, can we embrace the same attitude?

HELP ME FORGIVE AS YOU FORGAVE ME.

Into Your Hands

Then Jesus, calling out with a loud voice,
said, "Father, into your hands I commit my spirit!"
And having said this he breathed his last.
LUKE 23:46 ESV

Jesus was whipped, beaten, spit on, and given vinegar when He asked for water. His hands and feet were nailed to a rugged, splintery cross. Soldiers jammed a harsh crown of thorns on His head. There was probably blood in His eyes. He'd hung on that cross, struggling for breath, for six hours or more. At this point, when Jesus knew He was about to die, He quoted Psalm 31:5, where David trusted God even though Saul wanted to kill him.

What hard, torturous things are you facing? Can you, like Jesus and David, say, "Into Your hands I commit my spirit"?

IT'S EASY TO TRUST YOU WHEN EVERYTHING'S GOING WELL, LORD. BUT WHEN ALL IS GOOD, I OFTEN FORGET ABOUT YOU. RIGHT NOW, IN THE MIDDLE OF HARD THINGS, I PUT MY LIFE IN YOUR HANDS. I TRUST YOUR LOVE FOR ME.

Have Faith

When he heard that Jesus had come from Judea to Galilee, he went and begged Jesus to come to Capernaum to heal his son, who was about to die. Jesus asked, "Will you never believe in me unless you see miraculous signs and wonders?" The official pleaded, "Lord, please come now before my little boy dies." Then Jesus told him, "Go back home. Your son will live!" And the man believed what Jesus said and started home.

JOHN 4:47–50 NLT

While Jesus was at Cana, He performed a lot of miracles. An important man in another town heard about Jesus and traveled to Cana to ask Him to heal his son, who was about to die. Some might say it took faith to make that journey. . .but faith isn't the same as desire. The man came because Jesus was a last resort. He hoped. . .but hope still isn't the same as faith. It took *faith* for the man to go back home *without* Jesus, believing that Jesus would do what He said He would.

TEACH ME FAITH.

The True Bread

"The true bread of God is the one who comes down from heaven and gives life to the world." "Sir," they said, "give us that bread every day." Jesus replied, "I am the bread of life. Whoever comes to me will never be hungry again. Whoever believes in me will never be thirsty."

John 6:33–35 NLT

Small children are often very literal. They have a hard time thinking in abstract terms. When it comes to spirituality, even adults can have difficulty connecting the dots. When Jesus referred to the manna that God sent to the Israelites in the desert, the crowd asked for the same kind of bread, hoping for a lifetime supply of physical food. They missed the point entirely. Jesus told them, as He tells us, that He is the source of fulfillment, joy, peace, and love. He is the only one who can satisfy that emptiness inside us. When we come to Him, we'll never need to feel spiritually hungry or thirsty again.

FILL ME UP, LORD. I NEED YOU.

Back to Life

Then Jesus shouted, "Lazarus, come out!"

JOHN 11:43 NLT

All of John 11 sets up this moment, when Jesus called a dead man back to life. Unlike the children He saved, who were sick or had been dead only a short time, Lazarus had been dead four days. If anything was a miracle, this was! Lazarus obeyed the command, because even the dead must obey their Maker. Yet some of Jesus' harshest critics didn't take this as a sign that Jesus was God's Son. Instead, Lazarus' resurrection only made them more angry!

Do you need a miracle? Like Lazarus, are your God-given hopes and dreams dead and buried? What will it take for you to truly believe that God is who He says He is? What will it take for you to trust Him completely? Ask God to help you know and trust Him more.

FATHER, PORTIONS OF ME ARE DEAD. I NEED YOU TO BRING THEM BACK TO LIFE, BUT PART OF ME DOESN'T BELIEVE YOU WILL. TEACH ME TO TRUST YOU COMPLETELY.

Even If You Don't

"Now my soul is deeply troubled. Should I pray, 'Father, save me from this hour'? But this is the very reason I came! Father, bring glory to your name."
JOHN 12:27–28 NLT

The word *troubled* in this passage refers to turbulent waters. It reflects the anxiety that Jesus felt knowing what was in store for Him. He wasn't saying that He shouldn't ask God to save Him. In truth, He *did* ask God to save Him from what was to come when He prayed in the garden (Matthew 26). Yet, He pushed His own desires to the back, wanting God's purpose to be fulfilled.

It's okay to be anxious, as long as we don't stew in our anxiety. It's all right to ask God to save us from some dreadful circumstance, as long as we accept that God will use *any* circumstance for His glory. Be honest with God. Tell Him what you want. Then trust Him with the outcome.

SAVE ME FROM WHAT I'M FACING, LORD.
BUT EVEN IF YOU DON'T, I TRUST YOU.

The Heart Knower

Then they all prayed, "O Lord, you know every heart. Show us which of these men you have chosen as an apostle to replace Judas in this ministry, for he has deserted us and gone where he belongs."

ACTS 1:24–25 NLT

The phrase "you know every heart" comes from the Greek word *kardiognōstēs*, which means "heart knower." The early converts needed to replace Judas so they'd have twelve disciples again, and two men were up for the job. They asked God to make it clear which one—Matthias or Joseph—was the best man for the job. God has a specific plan and purpose for each of us. He knows our hearts and our thoughts, our abilities and our weaknesses.

We may want something for ourselves, but God sees what we cannot. He may have a different purpose for us. Or He may know that we wouldn't enjoy or do well at the thing we think we want. Trust His plan.

THANK YOU FOR BEING THE HEART KNOWER. I TRUST YOUR PLAN FOR MY LIFE.

The Beggar

But Peter said, "I don't have any silver or gold for you. But I'll give you what I have. In the name of Jesus Christ the Nazarene, get up and walk!"
ACTS 3:6 NLT

One day Peter and John went to the temple. At the temple gate, a man who'd been lame from birth was being carried there so he could beg. He asked Peter and John for money. Perhaps he held out his hand, expecting a few coins.

But Peter gave him something even better! In Jesus' name, he commanded the man to get up and walk. Peter helped the man stand up, and soon the man not only walked—he leaped and danced and praised God! What a difference a day can make.

God has so much more to give us than we can imagine. We often ask Him for just enough to get by. . .but He wants to heal us and strengthen us. He wants to give us joy. We ask for sustenance; He wants to make us prosperous.

HELP ME DANCE, JESUS!

God has so much
more to give us
than we can imagine.

Great Boldness

"And now, O Lord, hear their threats, and give us, your servants, great boldness in preaching your word. Stretch out your hand with healing power; may miraculous signs and wonders be done through the name of your holy servant Jesus."

Acts 4:29–30 NLT

The day before this prayer, Peter and John healed a man who'd been lame from birth. That caused quite a stir, and now crowds flocked to them to learn about this miraculous power. The Sanhedrin—the ruling council over the Jews—wanted to silence Peter and John. They had those two arrested but had to let them go because, what would they charge them with?

Peter and John prayed for boldness. They didn't pray to escape persecution—Jesus had warned them it was coming. Instead, they asked God to help them fulfill their mission and purpose despite the persecution.

FATHER, I DON'T WANT TO BE PERSECUTED OR OSTRACIZED BECAUSE OF MY FAITH IN YOU. IF AND WHEN THAT HAPPENS, HELP ME STAND FIRM AND LIVE OUT YOUR PURPOSE FOR MY LIFE.

Father, Forgive Them

As they stoned him, Stephen prayed, "Lord Jesus, receive my spirit." He fell to his knees, shouting, "Lord, don't charge them with this sin!" And with that, he died.

Acts 7:59–60 NLT

Stephen was the first Christian martyr. Stoning was a slow, cruel way to die. Before being executed, the victim was asked to admit to their crime. In this case, the crime was faith in Jesus. Instead, Stephen gave a long speech proclaiming Christ as the promised Messiah and condemning the Sanhedrin for standing in God's way. They were enraged!

Yet while they dragged Stephen to the cliff where they'd first push him over and then stone him, he prayed what Jesus had prayed on the cross—*Lord, forgive them.* Stephen knew his physical death wasn't the end for him. His concern was for all the people in the crowd who were physically alive but spiritually dead.

FATHER, OPEN MY EYES TO THOSE AROUND ME WHO NEED YOU.

Changed in a Moment

"Who are you, lord?" Saul asked. And the voice replied, "I am Jesus, the one you are persecuting! Now get up and go into the city, and you will be told what you must do."
ACTS 9:5–6 NLT

Saul was a devout Jew who, at the Sanhedrin's bidding, was determined to find every Jesus follower he could and bring them back to stand trial. It was his goal to kill Christians and shut them up for good. But on his way to find some more of these people, Saul was thrown to the ground and blinded by a bright light. He heard Jesus' voice clearly, and his life changed. God sent him to make disciples of the Gentiles, because if he had gone back home, he would have been arrested and killed for being a traitor.

God turned a killer of Christians into a Christian. No matter what you've done, God can turn things around. He's more concerned about your future than your past.

YOU KNOW MY PAST, FATHER.
MAKE ME WHO YOU WANT ME TO BE.

Praying for Friends

Beloved, I pray that all may go well with you and that you may be in good health, as it goes well with your soul.
3 JOHN 2 ESV

In this short letter, John wrote to Gaius, a man who had a stellar reputation for caring for missionaries. It appears John and Gaius had been friends for a while. John was an older man, and Gaius may have been too.

It's easy to get caught up in praying for our own needs. But prayer isn't meant to be self-serving. Yes, God wants us to tell Him our needs, our desires, and our concerns. But it's also important to lift up other Christians in prayer. We're all in life together, and when God blesses one of us, that blessing trickles to other believers. In this case, John wanted God to bless Gaius not only as a reward but also as security for future missionaries who would need the support of Gaius and others like him.

PLEASE BLESS MY CHRISTIAN FRIENDS.
KEEP THEM WELL AND SAFE.

You Are Worthy

"Worthy are you, our Lord and God, to receive glory and honor and power, for you created all things, and by your will they existed and were created."
REVELATION 4:11 ESV

In Genesis 1:1—the beginning of the Bible—we learn that God created the heavens and the earth. Now in Revelation—the end of the Bible—we're pointed back to this fact. Nothing on this earth would exist without Him. Hebrews 11:3 says the whole world was formed by God's word. Our mighty, awesome God spoke, and stars appeared. Planets appeared. *We* appeared.

Wow.

He is truly worthy of all good things, isn't He? He's worth all the glory and honor we can give Him. He's worth every bit of power we can attribute to Him. He's all of that, and still. . . He knows each of us by name. He loves us more than life. Sit a moment in that knowledge, and praise Him.

THERE ARE NO WORDS TO DESCRIBE HOW AMAZING YOU ARE, FATHER. I'M OVERWHELMED AT THE VASTNESS OF YOUR POWER, YOUR GOODNESS, AND YOUR LOVE.

Dramatic Rescue

"Worthy is the Lamb who was slain, to receive power and wealth and wisdom and might and honor and glory and blessing!"
REVELATION 5:12 ESV

In Revelation 5, John described a vision. He stood before God's throne, where a sealed scroll needed to be opened. The scroll represents God's judgment on our sin. But no one was worthy to open it! John wept at our lost cause. Without someone to intercede for us, we have no hope. Then one of the elders reassured John. "Don't cry. The Lion of Judah is worthy! He's the Lamb who was slain for our sins. He's got this!" Then Jesus opened the scroll, and heaven burst forth in loud praise, "Worthy is the Lamb who was slain!"

The passage is dramatic because what Christ did for us is dramatic. He died for us collectively. He also saved us *individually*. Jesus sees you. He loves you. And He has already rescued you. All you have to do is trust Him.

THANK YOU FOR MY DRAMATIC RESCUE, JESUS. YOU ARE WORTHY OF ALL MY PRAISE!

Overflowing Joy

And I heard every creature in heaven and on earth and under the earth and in the sea, and all that is in them, saying, "To him who sits on the throne and to the Lamb be blessing and honor and glory and might forever and ever!"
REVELATION 5:13 ESV

Do you ever wonder why God loves our praise so much? It's not only for His sake. It's for our sake too. When we delight in something, we praise it. *That was such a good book! I loved that movie so much. He is so handsome!* C. S. Lewis said that praise doesn't just describe our joy. It completes it. We praise something because we want others to join in, to agree with us. We want others to be as excited as we are.

In John's vision, every creature in existence praised God. When that kind of praise fills our hearts and minds, we overflow with joy and draw others to His love.

I PRAISE YOU WITH ALL THAT IS IN ME, FATHER!

One Day

He who testifies to these things says, "Surely I am coming soon." Amen. Come, Lord Jesus!
REVELATION 22:20 ESV

The Christian life brings a series of conundrums. We want to be with Jesus in glory, yet we want to live here. We want Him to come soon, yet we want all our friends and loved ones to know Him, and for that we need more time.

His return is already marked on the calendar, and only God knows the date. Until then, we must live our lives with the sincere purpose of loving Him and sharing that love with others. One day we will spend eternity with Him in a place more beautiful than we can imagine. At that point, it will be too late to introduce anyone else to His love. So find joy in living out that purpose now, knowing that soon we will see Him face-to-face.

I WANT YOU TO COME SOON, JESUS. BUT I ALSO NEED MORE TIME TO SHARE YOUR LOVE WITH THOSE I CARE ABOUT. MY LIFE IS YOURS.

Ask God

If any of you lacks wisdom, you should ask God, who gives generously to all without finding fault, and it will be given to you.

James 1:5 NIV

It's been said that God's Word addresses any problem we may face in life. That's not exactly true. The principles in God's Word can apply to any situation, but sometimes, things aren't black-and-white. Sometimes, we're left scratching our heads over which job to take, what city to live in, or even who to marry. When that happens, we should bury ourselves in prayer and ask God to guide us.

Sometimes He makes things obvious. Other times we have to lean in, straining to hear His voice. But He will always, always give wisdom and guidance to those who sincerely ask. Commit to standing still and not making a move until you're sure you've heard from God, and trust Him to lead you.

I NEED YOUR WISDOM, LORD.
I'M AT A CROSSROADS, AND I DON'T KNOW WHAT TO DO. LET ME HEAR YOUR CLEAR GUIDANCE. I'M AT A LOSS WITHOUT YOU.

On the Rock

"Therefore everyone who hears these words of mine and puts them into practice is like a wise man who built his house on the rock."
MATTHEW 7:24 NIV

As a child, you may have sung the song about the wise man who builds his house on the rock and the foolish man who builds his house on the sand. How does the song apply to our spiritual lives? The wise person builds their life on Christ, the Rock, while the foolish person builds on anything else. For the wise person, that connection with Christ is daily strengthened and solidified through the act of prayer.

Each day, the choices we make either build up or tear down. Make prayer a daily habit—not just once a day, but constantly throughout the day. Share every moment with your Father, seeking His guidance, giving Him praise, and living in the warmth of His love.

I WANT MY LIFE TO BE BUILT ON YOU, FATHER. WALK WITH ME TODAY. TALK WITH ME EACH MOMENT. I LOVE DOING LIFE WITH YOU.

Get Wisdom, Not Gold

How much better to get wisdom than gold,
to get insight rather than silver!
Proverbs 16:16 niv

Our culture encourages us to get gold—to get stuff, to get more, more, more of everything. Yet studies have shown that this kind of cycle leads to stress and anxiety, relationship issues, and health problems. The sad thing is more stuff doesn't bring happiness or joy. It just causes more clutter.

Minimalist theory touts the benefits of living with less stuff to make room for more of what's important. Proverbs 16:16 seems to agree with that theory: Stop trying to pile up more silver, gold, clothes, shoes, purses, cars—whatever. Instead, keep only what you need of material things, and spend your time seeking God's wisdom. In the process, you'll find more joy, peace, happiness, and love.

I'M SORRY FOR FOCUSING ON THE WRONG THINGS, LORD. I DIDN'T EVEN REALIZE I WAS DOING IT! HELP ME PURSUE THE LASTING WISDOM, JOY, AND PEACE THAT COMES FROM A CLOSE RELATIONSHIP WITH YOU.

Constant Thanks

I have not stopped giving thanks for you, remembering you in my prayers. I keep asking that the God of our Lord Jesus Christ, the glorious Father, may give you the Spirit of wisdom and revelation, so that you may know him better.

EPHESIANS 1:16–17 NIV

If we're honest, most of us spend more time thinking about what's for dinner or how to pay the bills than giving thanks for the people in our lives. Oh, we're glad they're there. But do we really thank God for them every day?

Paul did. He was so grateful for his friends in the Ephesian church that he *didn't stop* giving thanks for them. As he went about his business of making tents and writing letters and preaching sermons, they were in his heart. He asked God to bless them with wisdom, understanding, and a close relationship with God. Spend time today and every day asking God to bless your loved ones in the same way.

THANK YOU FOR MY FRIENDS AND FAMILY. DRAW THEM CLOSE TO YOU.

Listen to Advice

The way of fools seems right to them, but the wise listen to advice.

PROVERBS 12:15 NIV

Have you ever known a person who just wouldn't listen? Perhaps you've been that person. We all have, at some point. But most of the time when we go our own way without taking the advice of wise people, we regret it.

A key element in knowing who to listen to and what advice to take is spending time in God's Word and in prayer. True wisdom will never contradict God's Word. And the more time we spend with God, the more confident we'll be of His guidance—whether that comes through a scripture, a friend's words, or the Holy Spirit's still, small voice.

When we sincerely ask God for wisdom, He will give it. Ask God for wisdom today, and watch for the amazing ways that wisdom shows up. You won't be disappointed.

**I NEED YOUR WISDOM, LORD.
MAKE YOUR WAY CLEAR TO ME.
I WILL LISTEN AND OBEY.**

When we sincerely
ask God for wisdom,
He will give it.

True Beauty

Who is like the wise? Who knows the explanation of things? A person's wisdom brightens their face and changes its hard appearance.
Ecclesiastes 8:1 NIV

Have you ever known a person who just glows? When you're around them, you feel safe. You feel at peace. Though you can't put your finger on the reason, you want to be around that person. If they are a Christian, that quality is probably the Holy Spirit. God's presence in a person's life matures a person. It gives them wisdom and an inner light that can't be emulated.

The good news? That kind of beauty treatment is available to all who seek Him, all who make Him their first priority. Spend time with the Father today and every day, and let Him transform your spirit.

YOU ARE SO BEAUTIFUL, LORD. I WANT THE INNER BEAUTY AND LOVE AND LIGHT THAT COMES FROM A CLOSE RELATIONSHIP WITH YOU. SHINE YOUR LIGHT THROUGH ME SO OTHERS CAN SEE YOUR BEAUTY TOO.

Pray Always

Do not be anxious about anything,
but in every situation, by prayer and petition,
with thanksgiving, present your requests to God.
PHILIPPIANS 4:6 NIV

No matter who you are, you're probably bombarded with bills and family responsibilities and a million other things. It's hard to make time to pray. But prayer is essential. Prayer brings peace, while its absence brings anxiety. Prayer adds wisdom, but its absence leads to foolish mistakes.

Too often, we wait for things to get *really bad* before we "bother" God. But He *longs* for our presence. He wants us to talk to Him about everything. He is interested in each aspect of our lives, no matter how big or small.

Spend time in conversation with God as you drive to work or the grocery store, as you fold laundry, as you stir that pot of chili. Thank Him for His goodness, share your concerns, and rest in His presence.

I'M OVERWHELMED THAT YOU'RE INTERESTED IN ALL THE DETAILS OF MY LIFE, FATHER. THANK YOU FOR CARING ABOUT EVERYTHING I CARE ABOUT.

Casting Practice

Cast all your anxiety on him because he cares for you.
1 Peter 5:7 NIV

This is perhaps one of the most memorized verses in the Bible. It's embroidered on pillows. It's matted and framed, hanging in the entryway. It's been written into countless songs. But are we really doing what it says, or do we simply focus on the part where God cares?

If that's all we get from this verse, we're missing the point. The word *cast* is a verb. It's an action, and it requires us to do something hard. Picture yourself picking up a heavy stone and casting it as far as you can. That's what it feels like, sometimes, to cast our worries on God. We have to put some muscle behind it. It's not easy. It requires faith that He will catch them and take care of them.

He will, you know. He cares for you more than you can ever understand. Cast your worries, fears, and anxieties on Him, and rest in His love.

HELP ME CAST MY ANXIETIES
TO YOUR FEET.

Parting Gift

*"Peace I leave with you; my peace I give you.
I do not give to you as the world gives. Do not let
your hearts be troubled and do not be afraid."*
JOHN 14:27 NIV

When Jesus departed this earth, He didn't leave us empty-handed. He left some beautiful parting gifts. Unlike gifts that people give each other, His gifts won't wear out or go out of style. They are valuable and permanent. Peace is one of those gifts.

As Christians, peace already belongs to us. We don't have to search for it. . .we only have to access what's already inside us, through the Holy Spirit. That doesn't mean we won't ever feel anxious or afraid or angry. But we don't have to stay there. We don't have to live in chronic stress, for we have a Savior who wants to take it from us and replace it with the knowledge that He is good, He is in control, and He loves us beyond measure.

THANK YOU FOR YOUR PEACE, JESUS.

His Power in Us

For the Spirit God gave us does not make us timid,
but gives us power, love and self-discipline.
2 Timothy 1:7 NIV

When was the last time you felt intimidated? Look in the middle of that word, and you'll find *timid*. Maybe you're a naturally shy person, and big crowds make you feel timid and afraid. Or perhaps you're boisterous and outgoing, but certain situations make you uncomfortable. God wants you to remember that you're His child. By right of inheritance, He's given you a powerful persona. That power is strengthened through love and self-discipline.

Whatever the situation, hold your head high and your shoulders back. Keep a steady conversation with God in your mind. Treat others with love—there's power in that. Trust God to help you make the right choices—that's self-discipline. You belong to Him. His power lives in you.

REMIND ME OF THE POWER YOU PLACED IN ME, FATHER. HELP ME REPLACE TIMIDITY WITH CONFIDENCE. TEACH ME TO ACCESS THE POWER, LOVE, AND SELF-DISCIPLINE THAT COME FROM YOU.

Give your burdens to the LORD, and he will take care of you. He will not permit the godly to slip and fall.

PSALM 55:22 NLT

It's easy to take this promise out of context. We look at our lives and all the times we've slipped and fallen, and we wonder why God didn't intervene. It's important to ask a different question: Did we do our part?

We often walk around carrying burdens that we were never meant to carry, that are too heavy for us. They will surely trip us up. Then when we stumble, we look to God and say, "Why did You let that happen?" It wouldn't have happened if we'd given it to God to carry. Lay your burdens at His feet and leave them there. Don't pick them back up. Instead, hold His hand and let Him lead you through life's trouble spots.

I WANT YOU TO TAKE CARE OF ME, LORD. I ALSO WANT TO HANG ON TO MY TROUBLES SO I CAN TRY TO CONTROL THEM. HELP ME LEAVE THEM WITH YOU.

Confident in Him

So we can say with confidence, "The Lord is my helper, so I will have no fear. What can mere people do to me?"
Hebrews 13:6 NLT

When we look at our lives from a secular standpoint, people can make or break us. They can hurt us physically and emotionally. They can stand in the way of our goals. They can lie, cheat, and steal from us. None of those are pleasant possibilities.

But as Christians, our perspective is eternal. Christ helps us through life's hardships. Second Corinthians 4:9 tells us we may be persecuted, but we're never abandoned. We may be struck down, but we're never destroyed. We are more than conquerors in this life (Romans 8:37). There is nothing any human can do to us that will harm our eternal status. As for the temporary stuff, God gives us power. He guides and helps us. No matter what, we can be confident that we are on the winning team.

THANK YOU FOR HELPING ME. TAKE MY FEAR, AND GIVE ME CONFIDENCE IN YOU.

Strong and Courageous

"This is my command—be strong and courageous! Do not be afraid or discouraged. For the Lord *your God is with you wherever you go."*

Joshua 1:9 NLT

When Moses died, Joshua became Israel's new leader. It was an overwhelming task, and Joshua would have had every right to feel anxious about his new job. Yet God didn't just encourage Joshua. He didn't give a pep talk or a suggestion. He gave a command: "Be strong and courageous!"

God commands us to do the same thing. He is with us wherever we go. His Spirit lives inside us. When we wallow in our fears, anxieties, and insecurities, we deny the power of His presence.

What scares you today? What causes you stress? Remind yourself of this command: "Be strong and courageous!" He is with you wherever you go.

I WANT TO BE STRONG AND COURAGEOUS, LORD. BUT THAT KIND OF CONFIDENCE DOESN'T COME EASY FOR ME. REMIND ME OF YOUR PRESENCE. LIVE OUT YOUR POWER THROUGH ME.

Here and Now

"So don't worry about tomorrow, for tomorrow will bring its own worries. Today's trouble is enough for today."
MATTHEW 6:34 NLT

According to research at Penn State University, 91 percent of the things we worry about never come true. Of the remaining 9 percent, most of it isn't nearly as bad as we anticipate. Yet most of us worry about stuff all the time. With all that worry come health problems, relationship issues, and bad moods.

God wants us to ask ourselves, "Is everything okay in this moment?" If we have an immediate need, we can ask God and trust Him with the outcome. He loves to show off His power.

As for the rest—the stuff about the future that steals our peace—leave that with Him. Focus on the present. Spend time with your family. Enjoy nature. Give thanks for your car, your shoes, your job, and all the other things He's blessed you with, right here and now.

I'M SORRY FOR NOT TRUSTING YOU WITH MY FUTURE. HELP ME FOCUS ON TODAY.

Complete Trust

Trust in the L*ORD* *with all your heart; do not depend on your own understanding. Seek his will in all you do, and he will show you which path to take.*

PROVERBS 3:5–6 NLT

"Do not depend on your own understanding." Does this mean we're supposed to throw common sense out the window and do what feels right? Of course not. We use our intelligence and our experiences to gather information. But we're not to *lean on* that understanding, because some things will never make sense to our human minds.

When we seek God in all we do. . .when we spend time with Him in a constant prayer conversation. . .when we trust Him even when we don't understand, He makes the path obvious. Some translations say, "He will make the path straight." In other words, when we do our part, He will make it very clear what we're supposed to do.

I'M SORRY FOR PUTTING TOO MUCH STOCK IN MY OWN INTELLIGENCE AND EXPERIENCE. REMIND ME TO TRUST YOU MORE THAN I TRUST MYSELF.

Even when we can't see
any possible way out of
a situation, God will
often reveal a solution.

Answer to Prayer

I prayed to the Lord, and he answered me.
He freed me from all my fears.
Psalm 34:4 NLT

Just before writing this psalm, David was nearly captured by the Philistines. He surely would have been killed, and he saw no way of escape. Then in a dramatic move, David pretended to be insane. In that culture, those who were insane were considered to be possessed by evil spirits, and people wanted nothing to do with that. They didn't even want to touch David! As a result, David escaped. Here, in Psalm 34:4, he thanked God for helping him out of a hopeless position.

Even when we can't see any possible way out of a situation, God will often reveal a solution when we trust Him completely. He will also give us peace as we face our storms with courage, strength, and dignity.

I CAN LOOK BACK ON MY LIFE AND SAY WITH ALL CERTAINTY THAT WHEN I'VE TRUSTED YOU, YOU'VE NEVER FAILED ME. I KNOW YOU NEVER WILL.

Finding Joy

I pray that God, the source of hope, will fill you completely with joy and peace because you trust in him. Then you will overflow with confident hope through the power of the Holy Spirit.

ROMANS 15:13 NLT

Joy is one of those qualities that is hard to define. . .but we know it when we feel it! Joy encompasses happiness, delight, and pleasure. But it's somehow more than any of those things. Joy sinks deep below the surface and filters through to everything it touches. Too often, we equate joy with happiness, but happiness is always temporary. We associate joy with pleasure, but that too is fleeting.

Happiness and pleasure are based on our current circumstances, but joy is based on our future. That's why, as Christians, we can find joy even in the worst situations. We know that what we're going through is temporary. But God's love is eternal, and nothing can take it away.

I NEED YOUR JOY, FATHER.
FILL ME WITH YOUR PRESENCE AND
REMIND ME OF YOUR PROMISES.

Rejoice Always

Always be full of joy in the Lord. I say it again—rejoice!
PHILIPPIANS 4:4 NLT

This is one of those pretty verses that is easier said than done. How are we supposed to rejoice when we have a flat tire or we don't have money to pay our bills or we've been diagnosed with a dreaded disease? How can those circumstances be joyful?

They're not. But we don't rejoice *because of* our problems. We rejoice *in spite of* them. No matter what we experience, no matter what life throws at us, we are God's beloved children. He adores us so much that He sent Jesus to rescue us. And He's preparing a place for us so we can live with Him for eternity. Even now, in the middle of the chaos, He promises never to leave us or forsake us. Despite the storms, there's always joy in His presence.

TOO OFTEN, I FOCUS ON RIGHT NOW INSTEAD OF MY FUTURE. LET ME FEEL YOUR PRESENCE IN MY LIFE, FATHER. TEACH ME TO REJOICE!

Great Joy

Dear brothers and sisters, when troubles of any kind come your way, consider it an opportunity for great joy.

James 1:2 NLT

This verse goes against every ounce of common sense and human nature. How is hardship an opportunity for *great joy*? That's just silly.

Except, it isn't silly at all. The more impossible the situation, the more chance for God to show off. The more difficult the circumstance, the better the prospect for being more than conquerors (Romans 8:37).

Just as a bodybuilder must struggle to lift more weight in order to build muscle, we must struggle to experience growth. When we face trials, those are our opportunities to build spiritual muscle and become the fierce, powerful victors God created us to be. That's pretty exciting!

I DON'T ENJOY FACING TROUBLES, FATHER. I'D BE A LITTLE CRAZY IF I DID. BUT I KNOW EACH TRIAL IS AN OPPORTUNITY FOR GROWTH. I'M EXCITED TO SEE HOW YOU'LL USE THIS IN MY LIFE. TEACH ME TO FIND JOY IN EVERY CIRCUMSTANCE, KNOWING YOUR PLANS ARE GOOD.

The Sweetest Fruit

But the Holy Spirit produces this kind of fruit in our lives: love, joy, peace, patience, kindness, goodness, faithfulness, gentleness, and self-control. There is no law against these things!
GALATIANS 5:22–23 NLT

If you've ever had a garden, you know there's a lot of work involved. Even if the gardener does everything right, circumstances beyond her control can keep the plants from producing. But the Holy Spirit's garden always produces the sweetest fruit! We just have to remain connected to the Vine.

We connect to Christ through prayer, reading His Word, and doing His will. We connect to Him by doing the right thing, even when it's hard. We don't need to focus on the fruit—the Holy Spirit does that. All we have to concern ourselves with is keeping our connection strong. Soon, the fruit of the Spirit will show up, producing a beautiful array of God's character in our lives.

I WANT YOUR FRUIT TO BE ABUNDANT IN MY LIFE, LORD. REMIND ME TO STAY CONNECTED TO YOU.

In His Name

"Until now you have not asked for anything in my name. Ask and you will receive, and your joy will be complete."
JOHN 16:24 NIV

This is part of a speech Jesus gave to His disciples on the night of His arrest. He knew He was about to die. Before this, He'd never talked specifically about praying in His name. But now, He wanted His friends to know that there's power in His name.

We will sometimes ask for things that aren't in God's plan for us, and that's okay. Praying in Jesus' name isn't a blank-check formula that assures us that God will do what we ask. Instead, by praying in His name—by aligning ourselves with His will for us—we will receive the deep joy that comes from a strong, sincere faith. It's a lasting joy that trumps any temporary earthly pleasure.

I OFTEN PRAY WANTING YOU TO ANSWER ACCORDING TO MY OWN WILL. CHANGE MY HEART, LORD. I WANT TO PRAY IN YOUR NAME, ACCORDING TO YOUR WILL. THANK YOU FOR THE JOY THAT COMES FROM HAVING FAITH.

Good Medicine

A cheerful heart is good medicine,
but a broken spirit saps a person's strength.
PROVERBS 17:22 NLT

Have you ever stewed in your negative thoughts? We've all done that. Studies show that stress doesn't cause health problems; stress keeps us on our toes. Health problems come from *chronic* stress. The stressful thing happens, and we deal with it. But instead of moving on, we keep thinking about it. Each time we replay that negative event or emotion in our minds, our bodies respond as if it's happening in the present. When we do this, the stress of the event never goes away.

God has a better way. Don't think about the bad stuff more than you have to! Instead, follow the instructions in Philippians 4:8 and focus on what is true, lovely, noble, and right. Those happy thoughts are good medicine for the body, soul, and spirit.

I HAVE A BAD HABIT OF FOCUSING ON THE NEGATIVE, LORD, AND I KNOW IT'S NOT GOOD FOR ME. HELP ME SET MY MIND ON POSITIVE, HAPPY, JOYFUL THINGS.

Reason to Celebrate

Come, everyone! Clap your hands!
Shout to God with joyful praise!
Psalm 47:1 NLT

This verse is part of a song meant for worship. The writers invited *everyone*, not just the Israelites, to worship God with excitement and joy. Some scholars think this psalm was written after the Israelites overcame an enemy or after God saved them from capture. Whatever the occasion, it was a cause for celebration.

We can celebrate every day we live in communion with our Father, who loves us more than life. If you have a hard time thinking of reasons to celebrate, slow down. Consider your past and all God has done to show His tender care. Consider your present and all the ways He meets your needs. And consider your future, which will be spent in eternal celebration, basking in His presence and His love.

YOUR LOVE FOR ME IS REASON FOR CELEBRATION, FATHER! THANK YOU FOR ALL THE KIND THINGS YOU DO FOR ME EVERY DAY. EVEN WHEN I'M QUIET, MY HEART SHOUTS YOUR PRAISE.

Happy Hopes

The hopes of the godly result in happiness,
but the expectations of the wicked come to nothing.
PROVERBS 10:28 NLT

You've probably heard the phrase "Money can't buy happiness." Neither can ambition, goals, or material goods. Anything we can get on our own, without God, is temporary. And when we acquire those things by less-than-noble means, any victory is tainted. When we disregard God's ways, the pleasure is shallow and fleeting.

But when we set our sights on things above, when we align our goals and dreams and ambitions with God's purpose for our lives, He is pleased. He gives us contentment, happiness, and joy that we can find only through Him. What are your hopes? Do they align with God's desires for you? If yes, keep going down that path, and watch how He blesses you.

I WANT MY HOPES AND DREAMS TO LINE UP WITH YOUR PLANS FOR ME, LORD. I'M YOURS TO DO WITH AS YOU PLEASE. I LOVE THE JOY I FIND IN YOU.

Believing Without Seeing

You love him even though you have never seen him. Though you do not see him now, you trust him; and you rejoice with a glorious, inexpressible joy. The reward for trusting him will be the salvation of your souls.

1 PETER 1:8–9 NLT

Peter, the author of this passage, spent three years with Jesus. He ate with Him, laughed with Him, learned from Him. After Jesus died, Peter saw Him again, resurrected. His faith was based on eyewitness experience.

He marveled at his readers who loved Christ though they'd never seen Him. The same is true for us today. Peter pointed out that this kind of faith is special. This kind of faith is rewarded with salvation and a glorious, inexpressible joy.

Do you have joy in Jesus? It's there for the taking. Sink into His presence and be filled with His love.

I KNOW YOU'RE REAL BECAUSE I'VE MET YOU AND TALKED TO YOU. WE HAVE A RELATIONSHIP. I DON'T NEED TO SEE YOU WITH MY EYES. . . I KNOW YOU WITH MY HEART.

Trust and Wait

And my God will supply every need of yours according to his riches in glory in Christ Jesus. To our God and Father be glory forever and ever. Amen.

PHILIPPIANS 4:19–20 ESV

Have you ever woken up and felt like you needed coffee? Or chocolate? Our brains often confuse our wants with our needs. While we may not always get everything we want, God gives us what we need to live out the purpose He has for us. He meets our physical, spiritual, and emotional needs because He loves us and wants a relationship with us.

But He's not a bare-minimum God. He's not stingy with His blessings. If we open our eyes, we'll find that He gives us far more than we deserve, more than we could hope for or imagine. He has such good things in store for us. He is abundant with His grace, lavish with His kindness.

Never hesitate to tell God what you need. Then trust Him and wait to see how He blesses you.

YOU KNOW MY NEEDS,
FATHER. I TRUST YOU.

The Great Provider

"Look at the birds of the air: they neither sow nor reap nor gather into barns, and yet your heavenly Father feeds them. Are you not of more value than they? And which of you by being anxious can add a single hour to his span of life? And why are you anxious about clothing? Consider the lilies of the field, how they grow: they neither toil nor spin, yet I tell you, even Solomon in all his glory was not arrayed like one of these."

MATTHEW 6:26–29 ESV

One of our human flaws is that we waste energy on stuff that doesn't matter. One of our biggest time wasters is worry. Jesus pointed this out with a matter-of-fact rhetorical question: What good does it do?

Worry only steals our sleep and causes health problems.

God, on the other hand, will provide every needed thing for His children. And He provides in such a beautiful way! Do you trust Him?

THANK YOU FOR GIVING ME AND MY FAMILY WHAT WE NEED. I TRUST YOU.

God's Generosity

What then shall we say to these things? If God is for us, who can be against us? He who did not spare his own Son but gave him up for us all, how will he not also with him graciously give us all things?

Romans 8:31–32 ESV

When Jesus walked the earth, He taught us that the Father will provide for all our needs. In these verses, Paul reminded us of the same thing. If God is so generous that He'd offer His only biological Son to pay the ultimate price for our sins, why would He withhold lesser things? He is for us—100 percent, all-in, absolutely devoted to you and to me. There's *nothing* we need that He won't provide. And He's so generous, He also gives us a lot of things we don't need, just because He wants to bless us.

I CAN'T BEGIN TO COUNT THE WAYS YOU'VE BLESSED ME, FATHER. YOU'VE POURED OUT YOUR GENEROSITY IN BIG AND SMALL WAYS. I DON'T DESERVE THAT KIND OF DEVOTION, BUT I'M SO GRATEFUL FOR IT.

Bigger Things

Now to him who is able to do far more abundantly than all that we ask or think, according to the power at work within us, to him be glory in the church and in Christ Jesus throughout all generations, forever and ever. Amen.

EPHESIANS 3:20–21 ESV

Sometimes, life seems too big, too hard, too much for us. We carry the weight of our circumstances and those of our loved ones on our shoulders, and we wonder how long it will be before we collapse under it all. The reason this happens is simple: We were never designed to carry that weight.

God's power is unlimited. Through that power, He wants to carry all the heavy things for you. He wants to do bigger, more amazing things in your life than you can imagine. Your only job is to obey Him and submit to His will for your life.

I SURRENDER, LORD. I'M YOURS
TO DO WITH AS YOU PLEASE.
DISPLAY YOUR POWER IN MY LIFE.

God wants to do
bigger, more amazing
things in your life than
you can imagine.

Living Large

And he said to them, "Take care, and be on your guard against all covetousness, for one's life does not consist in the abundance of his possessions."

LUKE 12:15 ESV

Minimalism has gained traction in recent years. It's much more than a decor style. It's the conscious choice to keep only what's needed and not to hold on to excess. Research shows this lifestyle leads to lowered stress and more freedom.

Jesus taught about this way of life long before it was in vogue. God gives us abundance so we can share, not so we can hoard. He wants us to enjoy His blessings, not to store them in a closet. And He certainly doesn't want us longing for what others have while we're not even using what He's given us.

Stop comparing. Examine your own blessings. What can you pull out and enjoy? How can you bless others? Learn to live large by enjoying what you have, sharing with others, and immersing yourself in gratitude.

I WANT TO BE AN ABUNDANT GIVER, LIKE YOU ARE.

Clothes That Last

"For all these forty years your clothes didn't wear out, and your feet didn't blister or swell."
DEUTERONOMY 8:4 NLT

In Deuteronomy 8, Moses reminded the Israelites of the importance of keeping God's commands and serving Him only. He recalled the amazing things God did for them when He led them out of slavery in Egypt. One of the most impressive things was simply sustaining them for forty years!

Since they had to carry their belongings, they probably didn't have many changes of clothes or shoes. Yet in the forty years that they wandered in the desert, their clothes and sandals held up. Their feet didn't even get sore.

Whatever desert you're wandering through right now, trust God to sustain you. Talk to Him every day, and thank Him for all the ways He blesses you. He loves you, and He will see you through your journey.

THANK YOU FOR PROVIDING EVERYTHING I NEED TO KEEP MOVING FORWARD. I'M SORRY FOR COMPLAINING, WHEN YOU'VE BEEN SO GOOD TO ME.

What We Need

Oh, fear the Lord, *you his saints, for those who fear him have no lack! The young lions suffer want and hunger; but those who seek the* Lord *lack no good thing.*

Psalm 34:9–10 esv

In this passage, David used the word *fear* to mean "reverence" or "respect." David spent his early years as a shepherd, and we know that he killed at least one lion that was trying to attack his sheep. He knew that even strong, young lions get hungry. He also knew that God will take care of His children. Those who seek Him will lack no good thing.

That doesn't mean we'll get everything we want. God never promised that we'll live a wealthy, affluent lifestyle. But He will provide those things that are in our best interest. He will provide everything we need to serve Him well as we live out His plan and purpose for our lives.

THANK YOU FOR GIVING ME WHAT I NEED TO LIVE OUT YOUR PURPOSE FOR MY LIFE. I LOVE YOU, AND I TRUST YOUR PLAN FOR ME.

He Provides

I have been young, and now am old, yet I have not seen the righteous forsaken or his children begging for bread.

Psalm 37:25 esv

David wrote this psalm in his old age. His words were based on what he'd seen, not on every possible circumstance. There are certainly times when even the godly suffer hardship, war, and problems of every kind. But even in the most dire circumstances, God will never leave us or forsake us. Even in our darkest hours, God is right there beside us.

As a rule, God provides for His children. It may be in the form of a job that pays the bills. It may be through generous people or charities. And it may be through gentle surprises, such as a friend dropping by with a casserole when you didn't know what you'd feed your family for dinner.

Talk to God about your needs, and trust Him to provide.

FATHER, YOU KNOW WHAT I'M FACING. YOU KNOW WHERE I'M LACKING. I TRUST YOU TO GIVE ME EVERYTHING I NEED.

The Best Gift

"If you then, who are evil, know how to give good gifts to your children, how much more will the heavenly Father give the Holy Spirit to those who ask him!"

LUKE 11:13 ESV

Most parents try to be good parents. Even those who get it terribly wrong *usually* try to supply basic needs. They do their best to provide food and clothing for their children. So if even those with poor parenting skills try to do good things for their children, *how much more* will God—who is perfect, whose character is the very definition of love—give us something good?

The good gift Jesus refers to is the Holy Spirit—the best gift He could give us. When we have the Holy Spirit, we have God living inside us. He will never leave us, because He's part of us. He guides us and gives us wisdom every time we ask, because He's *right there*.

THANK YOU FOR THE HOLY SPIRIT. I'M SO GRATEFUL TO HAVE YOU HERE WITH ME.

In Love

Do everything in love.
1 Corinthians 16:14 niv

A few chapters earlier, in 1 Corinthians 13, Paul provided his readers with a beautiful, practical definition of love. It is patient, kind, honest, selfless. . . If you haven't read those verses, you should! Here, Paul circled back to that message. As Christians, every single action should be motivated by that kind of love. It's the way Christ lived His life. As His followers, we are to imitate Him.

When we're feeling annoyed or angry, it's still possible to act in love. It requires self-discipline. It requires setting emotions to the side and choosing actions that reflect love even when our feelings don't. But when we act in love, those feelings will often follow.

What do your actions communicate to those around you? What do your tone of voice and body language say? Ask God to help you communicate love in all things.

I DON'T ALWAYS ACT IN LOVE, FATHER. WHEN I'M UPSET, I OFTEN LACK SELF-CONTROL. I NEED YOUR HOLY SPIRIT TO HELP ME DO EVERYTHING IN LOVE.

Garden of Godliness

Love and faithfulness meet together; righteousness and peace kiss each other. Faithfulness springs forth from the earth, and righteousness looks down from heaven.
PSALM 85:10–11 NIV

Have you ever known a truly godly person who is faithful but not loving? How about righteous but stressed out all the time, with no peace? We all struggle with some of these attributes at times. But when we truly submit to God's will for our lives, when we truly honor Him in all we do, these qualities merge in a beautiful garden of godliness.

When we try to isolate these qualities, the results are incomplete. It's hard to be both loving and ungodly, or to be peaceful yet lack faith. It's only when we truly immerse ourselves in the Father, letting the Holy Spirit have complete control of our lives, that we can stand in the garden of love, faith, righteousness, and peace.

I WANT YOUR LOVE, FAITHFULNESS, RIGHTEOUSNESS, AND PEACE TO MERGE IN MY LIFE, LORD. I GIVE YOU FULL REIGN.

When Life Is Hard

Let the morning bring me word of your unfailing love, for I have put my trust in you. Show me the way I should go, for to you I entrust my life.

Psalm 143:8 NIV

When David wrote this psalm, he was in a bout of deep depression. He was tired of running from Saul. He was tired of defending himself when he'd done nothing wrong. He was tired of wondering if someone would kill him in his sleep.

Even though David went through such difficult times and struggled with his mental health, he kept up a constant communication with God. He shared his complaints and his blessings, his stresses and his praises. Here, he begged God to guide him and reminded Him of his complete trust.

We can learn much from David. No matter how hard things get, keep praying. Keep talking. And keep trusting. God is still writing your story, and the ending is beautiful.

GUIDE ME, LORD. LET ME HEAR YOUR VOICE. I TRUST YOU COMPLETELY.

Call to Action

"My command is this: Love each other as I have loved you."
John 15:12 NIV

We often equate love with a feeling or emotion. We get a warm, fuzzy sensation when we feel intense fondness for someone. But *love* is a verb. Its definition requires action, not emotion.

Christ loves us through action. When we continue in sin, He probably gets frustrated with us. That doesn't reduce His love. When we live in His will, He is pleased. That doesn't make Him love us more. His love for us was displayed on the cross, as He humbly gave His life in exchange for ours.

Most of us will never be called to give our lives for others. But we are called to be humble, kind, patient, and compassionate. Regardless of our feelings, we are called to act in love.

I CAN'T ALWAYS CONTROL HOW I FEEL, FATHER. BUT I CAN CONTROL HOW I ACT. THANK YOU FOR LOVING ME EVEN WHEN I'M HARD TO LOVE. TEACH ME TO LOVE OTHERS THE SAME WAY, THROUGH MY ACTIONS.

And now these three remain: faith, hope and love. But the greatest of these is love.
1 CORINTHIANS 13:13 NIV

In this verse, the word *remain* means "to last forever." Though some spiritual gifts will not be needed in heaven, faith, hope, and love will continue into eternity. It's through faith in Christ that we become part of God's family. Our abiding hope is that God has good things in store for those who love Him. Faith and hope are essential traits of Christianity. But *love* is the most important.

Nowhere in scripture are we told that God is faith or that God is hope. We have faith and hope in God. But 1 John 4:8 tells us that *God is love*. When we fail to love, we step in front of God and refuse to give Him access to our lives. But when we love, we allow God Himself to act through us.

I GIVE YOU FULL ACCESS TO MY LIFE, FATHER. LIVE YOUR LOVE THROUGH ME.

Choosing love takes self-discipline. But the payoff is great as we allow God to live out His character through us.

Choose Love

Hatred stirs up conflict, but love covers over all wrongs.
PROVERBS 10:12 NIV

We know that love is an action. Hate is also an action. Both of these are fueled by our feelings and emotions. Just as a car needs fuel to run, our actions are powered by the things we meditate on.

Thoughts are just thoughts. They're not facts. We can't control what flits through our minds, but we do have control over what we dwell on. If I have a hateful thought about someone, I can dismiss that thought and still act in love. But if I dwell on my ungodly thoughts, those ideas turn into actions. That hatred will spill into my attitude, my body language, and my tone of voice.

On the other hand, if I choose to focus on love, my actions will follow. Choosing love takes self-discipline. But the payoff is great as we allow God to live out His character through us.

I NEED YOUR STRENGTH TO HELP ME
HEFT ASIDE ANGRY, HATEFUL THOUGHTS.
I WANT TO DWELL IN YOUR LOVE.

A New Command

"A new command I give you: Love one another. As I have loved you, so you must love one another."
JOHN 13:34 NIV

The newness of Jesus' command isn't the *idea* of love. It's the depth of love. In the Old Testament, we're told to love our neighbor as we love ourselves. That's all fine and good. But Jesus says we're to love each other *as He loved us.*

Jesus loved us more than He loved Himself. He was self-sacrificing. He willingly gave up His life for us, in what He knew would be an excruciatingly painful, torturous death.

Most of us won't be asked to die for Him or others. But we are asked to *live* for Him. . .and for others. We're asked to pour out our lives for the sake of love. That's a hard request. But compliance with this command leads to a beautiful transformation of our spirits into God's image.

I DON'T KNOW HOW TO LOVE LIKE YOU LOVE, JESUS. BUT I WANT TO. LOVE THROUGH ME.

The Greatest Love

Greater love has no one than this, that a person will lay down his life for his friends.

John 15:13 NASB

When Christ said these words, He was preparing His disciples for His coming death. Dying a physical death for someone is the ultimate sacrifice. But laying down our lives for others shows ultimate humility.

Laying down our lives is as much of an attitude as an action. It means being humble and putting others' needs before our own. This isn't a popular concept in a me-first, look-out-for-number-one society. This kind of love puts our own desires on hold in favor of what others want or need. But the payoff is well worth the effort, because God sees and He is pleased. And He loves to bless those who lay down their lives for Him.

THIS KIND OF LOVE—SACRIFICIAL, HUMBLE LOVE—IS FAR BEYOND WHAT I'M CAPABLE OF ON MY OWN. I NEED YOUR HOLY SPIRIT TO TRANSFORM ME FROM THE INSIDE OUT. MAKE MY HEART LIKE YOURS, LORD.

First Love

We love because he first loved us.

1 JOHN 4:19 NIV

God calls us to love Him and others with a love that doesn't come naturally. God *is* love. The word *is* serves as an equal sign. We can never hope to truly love unless He is in us. And He would not be in us if He hadn't chosen to be. We are capable of love only because God chose to love us first.

The love He calls us to isn't just directed back to Himself. We're supposed to be His physical body here on earth. He shows His love to others through you and me. When we smile and offer a kind word, He loves through us. When we help those who can't help themselves, He loves through us. When we show mercy when we'd rather hate, His love wins.

When He chose to love us, He made it possible for us to love like He loves.

THANK YOU FOR TAKING THE FIRST STEP, FATHER. I'M SO GRATEFUL FOR YOUR LOVE IN ME.

Governing Authorities

Everyone must submit to governing authorities.
For all authority comes from God, and those in positions
of authority have been placed there by God.
ROMANS 13:1 NLT

God is the ultimate authority. He is Lord of all, and His power and rule are unmatched. Because of that, every authority here on earth is in place only because of God's design. That's a hard truth, especially when we don't agree with our authorities. Yet God's Word is clear: We are to submit to our government.

The only time we're not required to do this is when the government asks us to go against God's commands. In Daniel 3, when Shadrach, Meshach, and Abednego refused to bow before the king's image, God saved them from the fiery furnace. God will never hold us accountable for a law that goes against His Word. But for everything else, we must submit to the government and trust God to take care of us.

REMIND ME TO RESPECT THE PEOPLE AND INSTITUTIONS YOU'VE PUT IN PLACE, EVEN WHEN I DISAGREE.

The Coming Light

The people who walked in darkness have seen a great light; those who dwelt in a land of deep darkness, on them has light shone. You have multiplied the nation; you have increased its joy; they rejoice before you as with joy at the harvest, as they are glad when they divide the spoil.

Isaiah 9:2–3 ESV

In a dramatic act of faith, Isaiah chose to write about future events in past tense, as if they had already happened. He referred to the people who had rejected God; they walked in darkness. But he knew a time was coming when they would see the Light—Jesus Christ. One day, God would bless them and bring them joy.

In many ways, our world is in darkness still. But when we let Christ shine through us, we become the light! Pray, as Isaiah did, for the people around us to see the light of His love.

BLESS MY COMMUNITY, MY NATION, AND THE WORLD WITH THE UNDERSTANDING OF WHO YOU ARE. WE NEED YOU, FATHER.

Model Citizen

For the Lord's sake, submit to all human authority—whether the king as head of state, or the officials he has appointed. For the king has sent them to punish those who do wrong and to honor those who do right.

1 PETER 2:13–14 NLT

During the time that 1 Peter was written, Christians were hated. Many were falsely accused. Some believers may have grown resentful and thought, *There's no point in obeying the laws. I'm going to be punished anyway, so I might as well do what I want.* Peter warned his readers against such an attitude.

As Christians, we are to be above reproach. In other words, we're supposed to be model citizens as long as the laws don't contradict God's Word. If unbelievers are going to accuse us of wrongdoing, they'll have to lie.

Jesus showed this kind of submission when He willingly accepted His execution. He knew He'd done nothing wrong, and others knew it too. His attitude actually caused many to follow Him after His death!

HELP ME HONOR YOU BY OBEYING MY GOVERNMENT AUTHORITIES.

Pay Your Taxes

Pay your taxes, too, for these same reasons. For government workers need to be paid. They are serving God in what they do.

Romans 13:6 NLT

Every year at tax time, it's easy to complain about what we owe the government. And that complaint grows into criticism of all the government *isn't* doing, and how we shouldn't have to pay them when we're still suffering. But aside from some of the biggest names in Washington or our state capitals, most government workers don't make a lot of money. Their jobs are essential, but they work long hours for little pay.

Instead of complaining about paying taxes, try thanking God for the local, state, and federal government workers in your life. These include teachers, postal workers, social service employees, firefighters, police officers, and many more. Ask God to bless and protect these workers, and thank Him for allowing you to benefit from their services.

THANK YOU FOR THOSE WHO SERVE OUR COMMUNITY THROUGH GOVERNMENT JOBS. HELP ME BE A BLESSING TO THEM.

Movers and Shakers

So the L*ORD* *sparked the enthusiasm of Zerubbabel son of Shealtiel, governor of Judah, and the enthusiasm of Jeshua son of Jehozadak, the high priest, and the enthusiasm of the whole remnant of God's people. They began to work on the house of their God, the* L*ORD* *of Heaven's Armies.*

HAGGAI 1:14 NLT

It seems like many officials are great at making promises but not so great at keeping them. But God is all-powerful, and He is perfectly able to light a fire under those who can be movers and shakers in His causes.

However, we must play our part. He wants us to pray, believing that He will act. He wants us to speak kindly, even when we're frustrated. And He wants us to treat all people with love, even when we disagree with their actions. We often forget that even the government officials we don't care for are still just people who need Jesus.

WORK IN THE LIVES OF OUR GOVERNMENT OFFICIALS, LORD, SO THEY CAN DO YOUR WILL.

God's Government Servants

The authorities are God's servants, sent for your good. But if you are doing wrong, of course you should be afraid, for they have the power to punish you. They are God's servants, sent for the very purpose of punishing those who do what is wrong.

Romans 13:4 NLT

For a society to function well, there must be laws. We need people to enforce those laws. God has little tolerance for crooked, bullying authorities. If we must stand against these, we should always do it in the right way, with respect for the law and our legal system. After all, it's a system that God ordained.

Most government workers enter that service because they want to make a difference. We often hear about the bad eggs, but we must never discount the many others who sincerely want to help. We answer to God, and He requires us to follow laws and to respect authority.

I OFTEN FORGET TO PRAY FOR MY GOVERNMENT, LORD. BLESS THEM, AND MAKE YOUR LIGHT SHINE IN OUR LAND.

Doing What Is Good

Remind the believers to submit to the government and its officers. They should be obedient, always ready to do what is good.

Titus 3:1 NLT

Are we always ready to do what is good? In our society, we're encouraged to fight. Sarcasm, gossip, and negativity are often rewarded with coveted positions in the in-crowd. If we're *too good*, we risk being mocked.

But our goal isn't to please others or to be accepted by worldly people. Our goal is to please our heavenly Father and to shine His light in a dark world. It's hard to do the right thing, especially if you're the only one. Do it anyway. Speak kindly of that government official you can't stand. Show deference and respect to people in positions of authority. And always be ready to do what is good in God's eyes.

DOING THE RIGHT THING ISN'T ALWAYS THE POPULAR THING, LORD. REMIND ME TO STAND FIRM IN MY LOVE FOR YOU, EVEN WHEN THAT MEANS GOING AGAINST THOSE AROUND ME.

When Peace Reigns

For royal power belongs to the LORD. He rules all the nations.
PSALM 22:28 NLT

Right now, each nation has its own form of government. Some have republics, some have democracies, some have monarchies. But even the highest leader in each country answers to God alone. He is King of kings and Lord of lords. Nothing happens without His permission. Often, things happen without His blessing. But for now He's given us free will. And we humans often choose poorly.

One day Jesus will rule the entire world with an iron rod (Revelation 12:5). At that time, only those who rebel against Him will have reason to fear Him. His enemies will be destroyed, and the earth will be filled with peace, justice, and righteousness (Isaiah 9:7).

Pray for that day to come soon. In the meantime, ask God to shine His light through you.

I CAN'T WAIT FOR THE DAY OF YOUR RETURN, JESUS! I'M SO EXCITED FOR A TIME WHEN YOUR PEACE WILL REIGN. IN THE MEANTIME, LIVE THROUGH ME.

One day the earth will
be filled with peace,
justice, and righteousness.

Position of Influence

Daniel soon proved himself more capable than all the other administrators and high officers. Because of Daniel's great ability, the king made plans to place him over the entire empire.

Daniel 6:3 NLT

Daniel's life offers the perfect example of why Christians shouldn't fight against government. Instead, we should try to live above reproach. To the best of our abilities, we should never give anyone a reason to find fault with us. We should be honest, hardworking, kind, and wise. When we display this kind of character, we will outshine those around us. Even ungodly people will seek us out for help. Sometimes, like Daniel, we'll be placed in positions of influence.

Joseph is another example of this (Genesis 41:43). He had to go through some difficulties to get there, but he eventually became number two in charge of Egypt—a role that God used to save the nation of Israel. Ask God to make you capable, wise, and trustworthy and to use you however He needs.

SHAPE MY CHARACTER, LORD,
AND USE ME AS YOU WILL.

Seed of Faith

"The kingdom of heaven is like a mustard seed, which a man took and planted in his field. Though it is the smallest of all seeds, yet when it grows, it is the largest of garden plants and becomes a tree, so that the birds come and perch in its branches."

MATTHEW 13:31–32 NIV

Any gardener knows that the size of the seed doesn't determine the size of the fully mature plant. It's what's inside the seed that counts, along with the type of soil, the amount of water, and other environmental conditions.

When we believe in Christ, a seed of faith is planted in our lives. Inside that seed are all the elements of a strong, healthy, victorious relationship with God. Sometimes our environment can affect the shape of our lives. Though some things are outside our control, our choices matter. Are you playing your part in building a strong, vibrant faith?

THANK YOU FOR PLANTING A SEED OF FAITH IN ME. HELP ME WATER AND NURTURE IT INTO A STRONG TREE.

The Body

Instead, speaking the truth in love, we will grow to become in every respect the mature body of him who is the head, that is, Christ. From him the whole body, joined and held together by every supporting ligament, grows and builds itself up in love, as each part does its work.

EPHESIANS 4:15–16 NIV

Earlier, Paul wrote about the importance of using our gifts and abilities for Christ. It's like a physical workout. Our actions, not our desires, build a healthy body. When we use our gifts for Him, we (the church) become an incredible machine, each part working together to create a beautiful result: a world where Christ reigns. He is the Head. We are His hands, feet, heart, muscles, ligaments, and tendons.

Paul contrasts mature Christians with infants (verse 14). Infants and toddlers often throw fits when they don't get their way. He urged his readers, instead, to settle disagreements with love and to work together to accomplish His will.

HELP ME HUMBLY USE MY GIFTS AND ENCOURAGE OTHERS TO DO THE SAME.

Take Responsibility

Therefore, dear friends, since you have been forewarned, be on your guard so that you may not be carried away by the error of the lawless and fall from your secure position. But grow in the grace and knowledge of our Lord and Savior Jesus Christ. To him be glory both now and forever! Amen.

2 PETER 3:17–18 NIV

Peter finished this short letter by addressing his "dear friends." He cared deeply about his readers, and he didn't want them to be deceived by false teachers and to become insecure in their faith. Instead, he wanted them to dig down into the grace that God had already poured out on them and to grow strong.

As Christians, it's our responsibility to grow. We do that by learning more about Christ (head knowledge) and deepening our relationship with Him (heart knowledge). As we do, we'll recognize when someone tries to mislead us and others. Don't rely on what others have taught you. Own your faith, and take responsibility for it.

HELP ME GROW IN KNOWLEDGE AND GRACE.

More and More

And this is my prayer: that your love may abound more and more in knowledge and depth of insight.
PHILIPPIANS 1:9 NIV

In John 13:35, Jesus said that others will know we are His followers by the way we love one another. With that in mind, it makes sense that so many have turned away from the church. Sadly, many local church bodies are characterized more by bickering, gossip, and harsh judgment than by love. Who in their right mind would choose to be a part of that?

Centuries ago, Paul prayed for the Philippian church, and for us as well. He prayed that "[our] love may abound more and more in knowledge and depth of insight." To abound means to prosper and overflow. But Paul didn't want our love to overflow just a little. He wanted it to abound *more and more*—to keep spilling over.

THE MORE I KNOW YOU, THE BETTER I CAN LOVE OTHERS. LET YOUR LOVE SPILL OUT OF MY LIFE, ONTO THOSE AROUND ME.

Praying in a Crisis

"I loathe my very life; therefore I will give free rein to my complaint and speak out in the bitterness of my soul."

JOB 10:1 NIV

C. S. Lewis, in a letter to his friend Malcolm in which he discussed prayer, said we must "lay before Him what *is* in us, not what *ought to be* in us." Too often, we let our reverence for God turn into a negative kind of fear. We think He'll be offended if we say what we *really* think. But God already knows our every thought. We might as well be honest.

Job did this, in the middle of the crisis that stole his children, his health, his wealth, and his dignity. God expects nothing less from us. He wants our hearts—the good, the bad, and the ugly. He wants us to bring it *all* to Him, spew it out, and trust Him to clean up the mess. He loves us that much.

I HATE WHAT I'M GOING THROUGH. I DON'T UNDERSTAND IT. BUT I TRUST YOU.

The Exam

Examine yourselves to see whether you are in the faith; test yourselves.

2 Corinthians 13:5 niv

Comparison has become a sign of our times. In our spiritual lives, examining other people can be a pitfall. Instead of taking responsibility for our own sins, we look at others. *At least I'm not as bad as she is.*

Paul urges us to examine ourselves, not others. If we're not careful, we can end up patting ourselves on the back for having different struggles than those around us. But many times in God's Word we're told not to judge others. That's God's job! Instead, Paul encourages us to test our own hearts. Is God pleased with what He sees there?

Sometimes we know exactly where our trouble spots are. Other times, we need to ask the Holy Spirit to help us see our hearts clearly. Time spent in prayer shines a light on those areas and helps us get them in check.

SHOW ME WHERE I FALL SHORT, FATHER. I WANT TO BE LIKE YOU IN EVERY AREA OF MY LIFE.

Crave Nourishment

Like newborn babies, crave pure spiritual milk,
so that by it you may grow up in your salvation,
now that you have tasted that the Lord is good.
1 Peter 2:2–3 niv

Would you feed your minutes-old newborn a diet soda? Babies that young need their mother's milk or an appropriate formula. Everything about them is new, delicate, and fragile. They require the proper nourishment to grow strong and resilient. As they grow, proper nutrition will keep them healthy and allow them to resist illness.

Our spirits are no different. We are vulnerable to Satan's plans to pull us back into our old, sinful ways. We need to immerse ourselves in those things that will nourish our relationship with God. When we spend time reading His Word, praying, doing His will, and hanging out with other Christians, we gain the spiritual nutrition we need to resist sin and grow strong in Christ.

I DON'T WANT TO REMAIN A WEAK, IMMATURE CHRISTIAN. THANK YOU FOR GIVING ME ALL THE TOOLS I NEED TO GROW STRONG IN YOU.

A Long Fuse

You have planted them, and they have taken root; they grow and bear fruit. You are always on their lips but far from their hearts.

JEREMIAH 12:2 NIV

In the previous verse, Jeremiah filed a complaint. He asked God why the wicked are prosperous. Their prosperity comes from God; everything seems to go smoothly for them. Yet, though they say all the right "religious" words, their actions show that they don't care about pleasing God.

Several verses later, God assured Jeremiah that He knows. He sees it all. God is not short-fused, though; He gives His children many chances to repent and to make things right. But one day if their hearts remain hard, they will feel His judgment. Even then, He will always circle back to compassion for those who admit they've messed up and want a right relationship with Him once again.

SOFTEN MY HEART AND THE HEARTS OF EVERYONE I LOVE. LET OUR ACTIONS MATCH WHAT WE SAY WE BELIEVE. THANK YOU FOR YOUR PATIENCE, YOUR DISCIPLINE, YOUR MERCY, AND YOUR COMPASSION.

A Simple Prayer

The apostles said to the Lord, "Increase our faith!"
LUKE 17:5 NIV

What a simple prayer. "Increase our faith!" You'd think the apostles would have the strongest faith of anyone. They walked, ate, and camped with Jesus. They watched Him heal the blind and lame. They saw Him bring dead people back to life. Still, they each struggled to fully comprehend the magnitude of Christ's power.

We're no different. Time and again, God has worked miracles in our lives. He's delivered groceries when we had no food. He's given us a job when we needed one. He's given us good health and sustained us in poor health. Still, we struggle with faith.

We can grow in our faith by spending time with Jesus through prayer and learning His promises. It's our responsibility to do all we can to grow in Him, and to trust Him when we feel stalled. With the disciples, let's utter this simple prayer: Increase our faith!

I LOVE YOU WITH ALL MY HEART, LORD.
HELP ME LOVE AND TRUST YOU MORE!

Let my life
produce the fruit
of Your love.

Roots to Fruit

So then, just as you received Christ Jesus as Lord, continue to live your lives in him, rooted and built up in him, strengthened in the faith as you were taught, and overflowing with thankfulness.

Colossians 2:6–7 NIV

Healthy plants are evidence of a healthy root system. If you see an apple tree that produces sweet, juicy apples year after year, you can be confident that those apples don't just appear on their own. They're nourished from deep in the soil, where water and nutrients find their way through the tree. They're also nourished from a healthy dose of sunlight.

Christ acts as our roots and our light. If we remove ourselves from the soil of His presence or block His light from our lives, our faith will wither and die. But with the strong roots of prayer, Bible study, and God-centered action, we will grow strong, producing delicious, life-giving fruit.

THANK YOU FOR WATERING AND NOURISHING MY SPIRIT, FATHER. LET MY LIFE PRODUCE THE FRUIT OF YOUR LOVE.

About the Author

Renae Brumbaugh Green lives in Texas with her handsome, country-boy husband and two dogs. She teaches English and writing at Tarleton State University, writes a column for several newspapers, and writes books for children and grown-ups. In her free time, she does fun things with her four grown children and their amazing spouses, forces herself to exercise, reads historical fiction, and takes naps.